# Exploring Poetry 8-13

OTHER BOOKS BY BRIAN MERRICK

published by NATE


Exploring Poetry 5-8
(with Jan Balaam)

Talking with Charles Causley

# EXPLORING POETRY:
# 8-13

**Brian Merrick**

The National Association for the Teaching of English

Edited for NATE by Geoff Fox and Dennis Pepper
Design by Dennis Pepper

The photographs are by Brian Merrick and are of children working in the poetry lessons which were the source of this book. The captions are taken from the text.

First published May 1991

Published by The National Association for the Teaching of English, Birley School Annexe, Fox Lane, Frecheville, Sheffield S12 4WY

© 1991 Brian Merrick

ISBN 0 901291 19 6

First printed in England by Short Run Press Ltd, Exeter

# CONTENTS

Grateful thanks:

—   to Jan Balaam, Headteacher of Sidmouth County Infant School; at the time of the work described in Part One Section 3, East Devon Advisory Teacher for the Early Years

—   to Geoff Rickson, Graham Jones, Christine Hall and pupils at Honiton Primary School

—   to John Seal, Nick Price and pupils at St Peter's High School, Exeter

—   to Nadia Roberts and pupils at Ladymead Comprehensive School, Taunton

—   to Sally Holmes and pupils at Manor Junior School, Ivybridge

—   to Sean O'Shea and pupils at Bradley Rowe Middle School, Exeter

—   to Ken Saunders, Elena Dil, Bridget Rundle and pupils at Cheriton Fitzpaine Primary School, Devon

—   to Angela Cockerton, Sheila Grove, Maria Hussey, Lisa Jemphrey, Liz Kneebone, Matthew Lovett, Kate Parsons, Liz Quiney, Anna Russell, Lucy Watney and Alison Watts, and many other students at the School of Education, University of Exeter.


Special thanks:

to my wife Anne, who has accompanied me on many of my sessions in schools, made meticulous notes and transcriptions, and taken a major part in the whole project;

and to Geoff Fox and Dennis Pepper for unsparing help in editing and preparing this book for the printers.

## UNFOLDING BUD

One is amazed
By a water-lily bud
Unfolding
With each passing day,
Taking on a richer colour
And new dimensions.

One is not amazed,
At a first glance,
By a poem,
Which is as tight-closed
As a tiny bud.

Yet one is surprised
To see the poem
Gradually unfolding,
Revealing its rich inner self,
As one reads it
Again
And over again.

*Naoshi Koriyama*
Japan

# INTRODUCTION

This book is written in the belief that many teachers with some responsibility for language and literature do not see themselves as specialists in these areas and lack confidence both in their choice of poems and in their ability to generate enthusiasm for poetry.

The book offers guidance about providing a rich and pleasurable experience of poetry within the constraints of an ordinary classroom. The aim is to develop in young readers an enjoyment of poetry which may last through a lifetime. I like to think that the book will have many of the functions of an in-service course: if you work through all of the techniques it contains you will actually be equipping yourself to teach poetry in most circumstances you are likely to encounter.

My work at Exeter enables me to work with many poetry teachers, from those with long experience to students who may themselves have been pupils only one year before. This book is based on my own teaching together with what I have observed other people doing with poetry for children across the age range from 8 to 13. All of the suggestions made relate to actual practice: they have been 'classroom-tested'.

Three sections, 3, 6 and 9, relate mainly to the work of single teachers. The others draw on sessions taught by different teachers in different settings, or by myself. Sections 1, 4 and 7 focus on the work of a single poet.

The photographs record some moments of pupils and poems in evident 'engagement'. When we first encounter a poem it is as words that we hear or see. Whether these words come alive as a 'poem' depends for each of us on whether some form of engagement takes place. Most of us find that this is an individual matter and that someone else's explanation about what the poem means, or what is good or bad about it, is not in itself enough to bring the text alive.

Because each encounter with a poem is *unique*, we need to present poetry in circumstances which allow for a wide variety of 'entry points'. We also need to allow for the wide range of experiences, backgrounds and interests that the children in the class are bringing to the poem.

Those people who have pleasurable experiences of poetry at home or at school often associate the pleasure not merely with the qualities of the poems themselves, the words, the content, the shape, the sound, but with the circumstances in which each was enjoyed. Those circumstances frequently include other activities: dancing, singing, miming, chanting, beating out the rhythm on the arm of a chair or someone's knee; later they may talk about it, write, paint, draw, cut out shapes and glue them onto a background . . . the richness of the experience is often reflected by the detail with which it can be recalled, sometimes years later.

The approach to poetry teaching followed by all the contributors to this book acknowledges the necessity for:

1   the availability of a wide range of poetry books from which the teacher and pupils can select poems that appeal to them.

2   the introduction of each poem in a manner that allows the words on the page to come to life.

I am greatly indebted to Jan Balaam, whose poetry classes with 5–8 year olds I shared over a period of two years in our writing of *Exploring Poetry: 5–8* (NATE, 1987). The present book extends the philosophy and practice of poetry teaching described in its predecessor and adopts the same format. It is divided into three parts.

PART ONE consists of ten sections. An introduction giving the reasons for this particular selection is followed by the full text of the poems used. Teaching suggestions follow under three headings: *First Encounters, Developments* and *Further Developments.*

The *First Encounter* most often will be a reading by the teacher, though other possibilities are suggested. It is crucial that readers, whether adults or children, should themselves have previously experienced pleasure from the poem. If some way other than reading the poem aloud is chosen it should be calculated to arouse a positive response to a later reading.

*Developments* link the poem(s) to other activities the pupils may already enjoy and feel easy with. Many teachers need no advice about how to encourage discussions, set up role play, make collages . . . For this reason the suggestions are given without elaboration. Other readers may welcome advice and for them PART TWO deals with approaches to activities that have been suggested.

The developments of the first encounter are to provide openings for pupils to formulate, refine and give expression to their sense of the poem. This includes providing opportunity for exchanging opinions and insights as they carry out shared activities. In this way they transform the poem from words on the page into felt experience.

There will be occasions when the first response from a class to a poem deters a teacher from going any further with it. By contrast there may be occasions when a class develops a growing enthusiasm and wants to pursue a poem further and in different ways. For this contingency in each section some *Further Developments* are suggested.

Where it is appropriate, sections conclude with a list of *Related Poems* which might lend themselves to a similar approach, and indicate one book from those listed in PART THREE in which each may be found.

Because numbering would imply an intended sequence separate activities are signalled thus ★. The suggestions may often be most useful if they spark off ideas of your own, and certainly will be more successful if adapted to suit your own circumstances and practice.

It needs confidence to decide what poems a group of pupils, or even one pupil, will enjoy. It also needs access to a range of the many collections and anthologies that are on the market.

There are two separate problems:
—  deciding which poems are likely to succeed.
—  finding the poem.

The introduction to each of the sections in PART ONE sets out to answer the question, *Why this poem?* PART TWO Section 2 takes this further by laying down some guiding principles in making choices.

PART THREE contains lists of poetry books appropriate for the age range 8–13 currently available at a reasonable price. These are divided into 'collections' appropriate as the contents of a class or school Poetry Book Box.

A welcome effect of the National Curriculum should be a significant increase in the attention given to literature from other times and other places. I have set out to reflect this within this book.

PART ONE

SECTION 1

*ask for a story*

We begin deliberately with a section devoted to one of the great poets for adults and children. Walter de la Mare's poems work through the imagination, the sense of mystery and magic present in us all. The words, the sounds, the rhythm, the images, the subject matter and the simplicity draw readers into a world outside contemporary reference but one which they may have glimpsed through dream and story. They are poems which delight more with every fresh hearing. They invite a response from whoever is listening. They are poems to live with and return to again and again.

We often choose poems in school not only for themselves but for their connections. What they have in common may be the author, a theme, a setting, characters, a subject, a mood, an atmosphere, or even 'period'. Or they may have all of these in common, as in the case of the poems chosen here.

There is a distinctive voice speaking in each of the first two poems, and there are good reasons for using each to illuminate the other. It would be reasonable to treat them as a pair and then to move on. But if the magical spell that de la Mare can weave over attentive readers is having its effect, you might go one stage further, and introduce 'The Listeners'. 'Some One' and 'The House' make a fine preparation.

—◦◉◦—

## SOME ONE

Some one came knocking
    At my wee small door;
Some one came knocking,
    I'm sure – sure – sure;
I listened, I opened,
    I looked to left and right,
But nought there was a-stirring
    In the still dark night;
Only the busy beetle
    Tap-tapping in the wall,
Only from the forest
    The screech-owl's call,
Only the cricket whistling
    While the dewdrops fall,
So I know not who came knocking
    At all, at all, at all.

14

## THE HOUSE

A lane at the end of Old Pilgrim Street
Leads on to a sheep-track over the moor,
Till you come at length to where two streams meet,
The brook called Liss, and the shallow Stour.

Their waters mingle and sing all day —
Rushes and kingcups, rock and stone;
And aloof in the valley, forlorn and grey,
Is a house whence even the birds have flown.

Its ramshackle gate swings crazily; but
No sickle covets its seeding grass;
There's a cobbled path to a door close-shut;
But no face shows at the window-glass.

No smoke wreathes up in the empty air
From the chimney over its weed-green thatch;
Briar and bryony ramble there;
And no thumb tirls at the broken latch.

Even the warbling water seems
To make lone music for none to hear;
Else is a quiet found only in dreams,
And in dreams this foreboding, though not of fear.

Yes, often at dusk-fall when nearing home —
The hour of the crescent and evening star —
Again to the bridge and the streams I come,
Where the sedge and the rushes and kingcups are:

And I stand, and listen, and sigh — in vain;
Since only of Fancy's the face I see;
Yet its eyes in the twilight on mine remain,
And it seems to be craving for company.

## THE LISTENERS

'Is there anybody there?' said the Traveller,
     Knocking on the moonlit door;
And his horse in the silence champed the grasses
     Of the forest's ferny floor:
And a bird flew up out of the turret,
     Above the Traveller's head:
And he smote upon the door again a second time;
     'Is there anybody there?' he said.
But no one descended to the Traveller;
     No head from the leaf-fringed sill
Leaned over and looked into his grey eyes,
     Where he stood perplexed and still.
But only a host of phantom listeners
     That dwelt in the lone house then
Stood listening in the quiet of the moonlight
     To that voice from the world of men:
Stood thronging the faint moonbeams on the dark stair,
     That goes down to the empty hall,
Hearkening in an air stirred and shaken
     By the lonely Traveller's call.
And he felt in his heart their strangeness,
     Their stillness answering his cry,
While his horse moved, cropping the dark turf,
     'Neath the starred and leafy sky;
For he suddenly smote on the door, even
     Louder, and lifted his head:—
'Tell them I came, and no one answered,
     That I kept my word,' he said.
Never the least stir made the listeners,
     Though every word he spake
Fell echoing through the shadowiness of the still house
     From the one man left awake:
Ay, they heard his foot upon the stirrup,
     And the sound of iron on stone,
And how the silence surged softly backward,
     When the plunging hoofs were gone.

## FIRST ENCOUNTERS

★     **i**   Begin by talking with the whole class about experiences of being alone – maybe starting off with one of your own. Invite personal anecdotes, which may combine what really happened with what was imagined at the time. [This could arouse a strong response. Given sufficient time, and with encouragement, it could lead to extended story-telling, writing, illustration . . . which might run alongside your work on the poems. Don't delay the introduction of the poems for too long.]

    **ii**   Read 'Some One' to the class. Give careful thought to how you will read it. (See Part II Section 3.) Try it aloud *before* you read it to an audience. (This applies to any poem.)

    **iii**   Invite first reactions before distributing copies of the poem for them to read to themselves. Both of these activities should be unhurried.

    **iv**   Talk about the steps you took to find the voice for your reading. Invite one or two rehearsed readings from volunteers in the class. (Maybe in a later session, maybe after five minutes preparation time in pairs or threes . . .)

    **v**   Invite further discussion, leading to:
    **a**   comparing and contrasting the experience of the speaker in the poem with the experiences that arose in their personal anecdotes.
    **b**   deciding how the 'telling' in the poem differs from their own 'tellings'.

★     **i**   Read 'The House' to the class. Find an appropriate 'voice' for the poem. (See Part II Section 3.)

    **ii**   Invite first reactions before distributing copies for them to read to themselves.

    **iii**   Invite further comments or second thoughts. If necessary, ask some opening questions:
—  without looking back at it can they recall any words, pictures, or sounds?
—  any puzzling words or lines?
—  what do they feel sure/unsure about?
—  is there a voice *telling* this poem?
—  any connections between this and 'Some One'?

    **v**   Talk about the decisions you made in choosing the 'voice' for this reading. Allow time for preparation in pairs or individually, then invite readings by volunteers in the class.

★      **i** Distribute copies of 'The Listeners' and then read it aloud.

**ii** Introduce a second reading by someone else: a prepared pupil, one recorded for the occasion by another member of the staff . . . Request a few minutes silence at the end of this reading while everyone writes down at least three simple statements, no matter if they seem obvious, and/or three simple questions about the poem. The statements and the questions may be either about details or overall impact.

**iii** Use these as a basis for discussion, beginning in groups of four or five, later opening it up to the full class for their response to it.


## DEVELOPMENTS

★      **i** Discuss the qualities of a good reading of a poem. (See Part II Section 3.)

**ii** Divide the class into small groups. Ask each group to *collaborate* in preparing a good reading of any one of the de la Mare poems. Ensure that all three poems are covered.

**iii** Listen to a sample of the readings and if the previous work on prepared readings has been covered, talk about how they measure up to what the class decided earlier. Any really good readings might be recorded for playing another time.

★      In relation to whichever poem they have worked on, ask each group to consider which of the following the poem gives:
> pictures in the head
> a mood
> a story
> something else

and which, if any, is most powerfully conveyed.

★      **i** Provide everyone in the class with a personal copy of any one of the poems which they can keep, write notes on, and add to their personal poetry file.

**ii** Ask for silent readings of the poem, interrupted by unhurried pauses for noting on the sheet anything striking, puzzling, pleasing, irritating . . . The notes might take the form of jottings, arrows, sketches, full statements – whatever seems most appropriate to record the response or comment. (See Part II Section 6.)

18

**iii**  Before they finish, suggest that – if they haven't already done so – they should note points at which there is any kind of change in the poem.

**iv**  Divide into small groups of three or four according to the poem chosen to compare and discuss the notes they have made.

**v**  Bring all groups back together. Listen to a reading of each of the three poems, followed by the reports from each group on the points which aroused most agreement or disagreement in their discussion.

★  (*See* Part II Section 17.) Individually, in pairs or groups of three, working on any *one* of the poems:

**i**  Provide materials for an illustrated poster which includes the full poem, handwritten, combined with a visual image or images appropriate to its content. (Talk about the choice of colours to be used – the possible link, for instance, between colour and mood.)

**ii**  Arrange for a visitor to view the resulting display and, with all the class helping, to question the makers of each poster about their final product and the decisions they had to make.

## FURTHER DEVELOPMENTS

★  **i**  Re-read 'The House'.

**ii**  Talk the class back in time to when the house of the poem was occupied. Leave generous time for thought and jottings. (See Part II Section 8.)

**iii**  Ask for five minutes of fast, unedited writing about the individual people living in the house at that time.

**iv**  Ask for a story about the house, either when it was flourishing, or at the time when it was first abandoned.

★  **i**  Write questions relating to 'The Listeners' on the board (or better, on an acetate sheet for the O.H.P.) They should not be on show when the class comes into the room. Keep the questions focussed on the role within the poem of the Traveller. For example:
— where did the Traveller come from?
— what sort of person is he?
— what was his connection with the house in the woods before the poem begins?

19

— why had he promised to return there?
— where does he go at the end of the poem?
— how is he affected by the experience described in the poem?
Have these ready for display at the appropriate moment later in the lesson.

   **ii**   When the class comes in re-read 'The Listeners'.

   **iii**   Ask them to write down – individually – a list of questions about the Traveller that the poem leaves to the reader's imagination.

   **iv**   Listen to the questions they have noted before revealing your own list. Discuss how they compare.

   **v**   Ask for a story about the Traveller *or* an extended extract from a detailed diary that he keeps, either *leading up to* or *following on from* his experience in the poem.
(This activity might alternatively, or subsequently, be focussed on the role of the Listeners.)


## SOME OTHER RELATED PAIRS AND TRIOS


'Old Shellover' – Walter de la Mare *Secret Laughter* Puffin.
'Worms and the Wind' – Carl Sandburg in *Wordscapes* (ed. Barry Maybury)
    O.U.P.
'Hedgehog' – Clive Sansom (see Section 5).


'Thunder' – Walter de la Mare *Secret Laughter* Puffin.
'The Sands of Dee' – Charles Kingsley in *Oxford Book of Poetry for Children*
    (ed. Edward Blishen) O.U.P.


'Bully Night' – Roger McGough *In the Glassroom* Cape.
'The Forest of Tangle' – Charles Causley in *Collected Poems 1951–75*
    Macmillan
'Not Me' – Shel Silverstein *A Light in the Attic* Cape.


'First Snow', 'A Ghost Story', 'The Cry' – John Mole *The Mad Parrot's
    Countdown* Peterloo Poets.

*their judgments
can be illuminating*

A poem looks closely. It has a penetrating vision that offers a listener – or a reader – a fresh and illuminating experience, even of very familiar subjects. The best poems are expressed with vigour and extreme economy of language within a form which seems perfectly suited to the subject.

For me, each of the poems in this section demonstrates all of these qualities. The approach in each is quite different. But an element in my response is a sense of the complete success with which the poet has captured the subject within the poem.

## PRAISE OF A COLLIE

She was a small dog, neat and fluid —
Even her conversation was tiny:
She greeted you with bow, never bow-wow.

Her sons stood monumentally over her
But did what she told them. Each grew grizzled
Till it seemed he was his own mother's grandfather.

Once, gathering sheep on a showery day,
I remarked how dry she was. Pollochan said, 'Ah,
It would take a very accurate drop to hit Lassie.'

And her tact — and tactics! When the sheep bolted
In an unforeseen direction, over the skyline
Came — who but Lassie, and not even panting.

She sailed in the dinghy like a proper sea-dog.
Where's a burn? — she's first on the other side.
She flowed through fences like a piece of black wind.

But suddenly she was old and sick and crippled . . .
I grieved for Pollochan when he took her a stroll
And put his gun to the back of her head.

*Norman MacCaig*


## UNTIL I SAW THE SEA

Until I saw the sea
I did not know
that wind
could wrinkle water so.

I never knew
that sun
could splinter a whole sea of blue.

Nor
did I know before,
a sea breathes in and out
upon a shore.

*Lilian Moore*

## I'M A PARROT

I'm a parrot
I live in a cage
I'm nearly always
in a vex-up rage

I used to fly
all light and free
in the luscious
green forest canopy

I'm a parrot
I live in a cage
I'm nearly always
in a vex-up rage

I miss the wind
against my wing
I miss the nut
and the fruit picking

I'm a parrot
I live in a cage
I'm nearly always
in a vex-up rage

I squawk I talk
I curse I swear
I repeat the things
I shouldn't hear

I'm a parrot
I live in a cage
I'm nearly always
in a vex-up rage

So don't come near me
or put out your hand
because I'll pick you
if I can

    pickyou
    pickyou
    if I can

I want to be free

CAN'T YOU UNDERSTAND

*Grace Nichols*


## HEDGEHOG

His back's all prickles, but his pointed face
Is furry and his soft black-leather snout
Gentle and wrinkled. Sunlong in a ditch
He dozes on dead leaves, till with the dusk
He clambers out, shambling through twilight lanes
To scrabble banks for worms. When Autumn brings
The first cold winds, he'll find a rabbit hole
And, curled within it, sleep the snow away
Till March comes round to wake him. Then he'll crawl
Out to the sunbright rim of the world, and stretch
Dazzled and dreaming. But if danger's near
Up go his bristles, and he'll roll himself
Tight as a ball, tough as a blackthorn hedge!

*Clive Sansom*

## FIRST ENCOUNTERS

★      **i** With the full class/group look at one poem at a time, in any order, but treating each one with undivided attention for as long as the level of interest in it remains high. Allow time for hearing the poem read aloud, for individual silent reading and, if necessary, for reading in pairs.

      **ii** Follow these unhurried readings with an invitation for first responses. As a basis for discussion you might ask, *How does the poem match your own view of the subject?* and allow a few minutes for silent jotting in response to the question before anyone talks.

★      Introduce any one of the poems, or each one in sequence, by giving the class the title and allowing five minutes for writing some sentences of their own on whatever the title suggests to them. They might also list some comparisons that they might use if they were wanting to bring the subject alive in the reader's imagination.

Allow time for discussing these jottings before going on to read and to look at the poem.

★      After reading any of the poems to the class for the first time, allow further time for silent reading and for writing down any words or lines which they find difficult, strange or in any way remarkable or pleasing. Listening to these will lead naturally into discussion of the poem. Hearing comments from others in the class will demonstrate that their judgements can be as illuminating as the teacher's.

## DEVELOPMENTS

★      **i** Divide the class into small groups.

      **ii** Give each person in the group a sheet of paper, at least A4 size, to fold once lengthwise and once widthwise.

      **iii** Ask them to listen while you read one of the poems and to pay particular attention to the pictures which come into their heads.

      **iv** Request rapid sketches, one in each section of their folded paper, of any four pictures the poem created for them. Allow no more than 10 minutes for this and stress that no great artistic skill is expected!

**v** Looking back at the poem they should now choose a short quotation to go with each sketch – either working it into the drawing or using it as a caption.

For the next task they need to decide which of their four sketches captures the poem best or which most interests them. The comments of other members of the group can be helpful in making this choice. Once the decision is made they should consider how to improve the drawing. (See Part II Section 20.)

**vi** On a fresh A4 or larger sheet of drawing paper each one should now make a 'finished' picture, complete with its quotation.

**vii** The end results might be shown to the whole class and discussed. They might also be displayed in the classroom under a large heading showing the title of the poem and the name of the poet.

★     **i** Listen to readings of the four poems. Ask the class, either individually or in groups of 2 or 3, to look at the way the poets combine still pictures and moving pictures.

    **ii** Choosing any one of the poems ask them to list all of the still pictures and all of the moving pictures and be prepared to discuss:
        **a** What the moving pictures tell the reader that the still ones don't, and vice-versa.
        **b** which, if any, of the still pictures *imply* movement.


## FURTHER DEVELOPMENTS

★     Ask everyone in the class to choose one of the poems to learn by heart: the most effective of all ways of making a poem your own.

[You might fix a time for a classroom performance of the learnt poems, though participation might be optional. This could lead to a programme, by those willing, or a number of programmes consisting of one reading of each of the four poems, for performance to other classes.]

★     **i** Ask everyone to jot down a maximum of – say – 5 separate words from one of the poems, which they consider to be most effective in capturing the subject.

    **ii** When all are ready, divide into groups to compare the words chosen and talk about them:

— which did they all agree on?
— what do they tell you?
— what is strong about them?

**iii** If that works well and the level of interest seems high, go on to another of the poems.

**iv** At the point when you feel interest is flagging, draw the class together and listen to reports from the groups for each poem considered.

## RELATED POEMS

'The Man with the Wooden Leg' – Katherine Mansfield *Poems of Katherine Mansfield* O.U.P.

'Yesterday he was nowhere to be found' and 'The Cow is but a bagpipe' – Ted Hughes *What is the Truth?* Faber.

'I Like to Stay Up' – Grace Nichols *Come on into my Tropical Garden* A. & C. Black.

'Adlestrop' – Edward Thomas *Selected Poems of Edward Thomas* Faber.

'It was a long time ago' – Eleanor Farjeon *Something I Remember* Puffin.

Jan Balaam writes:

   The poems in this section speak directly to children through their own experience. They may be appreciated by each child on more than one level and many responses may be uniquely personal.

   Starting from the familiar activities included in the playground poems, children can be led further to explore sensitive underlying issues which relate directly to them, as in the two poems concerned with bullying.

   The four poems may be used together or worked on individually, according to the interests and needs of the group.

## WINTER

On Winter mornings in the playground
The boys stand huddled,
Their cold hands doubled
Into trouser pockets.
The air hangs frozen
About the buildings
And the cold is an ache in the blood
And a pain on the tender skin
Beneath finger nails.
The odd shouts
Sound off like struck iron
And the sun
Balances white
Above the boundary wall.
I fumble my bus ticket
Between numb fingers
Into a fag,
Take a drag
And blow white smoke
Into the December air.

*Gareth Owen*

## OUT OF SCHOOL

Four o'clock strikes,
There's a rising hum,
Then the doors fly open,
The children come.

With a wild cat-call
And a hop-scotch hop
And a bouncing ball
And a whirling top,

Grazing of knees,
A hair-pull and a slap,
A hitched-up satchel,
A pulled-down cap,

Bully boys reeling off,
Hurt ones squealing off,
Aviators wheeling off,
Mousy ones stealing off,

Woollen gloves for chilblains,
Cotton rags for snufflers,
Pigtails, coat-tails,
Tails of mufflers,

Machine-gun cries,
A kennelful of snarlings,
A hurricane of leaves,
A treeful of starlings,

Thinning away now
By some and some,
Thinning away, away,
All gone home.

*Hal Summers*

## FOUR O'CLOCK FRIDAY

Four o'clock, Friday, I'm home at last
Time to forget the week that has passed.

On Monday, at break, they stole my ball
And threw it over the playground wall.

On Tuesday morning, I came in late,
But they were waiting behind the gate.

On Wednesday afternoon, in games
They threw mud at me and called me names.

Yesterday, they laughed after the test
'Cause my marks were lower than the rest.

Today, they trampled my books on the floor
And I was kept in, because I swore.

Four o'clock, Friday, at last I'm free.
For two whole days they can't get at me.

*Derek Stuart*

## THE BULLY ASLEEP

One afternoon, when grassy
Scents through the classroom crept,
Bill Craddock laid his head
Down on his desk, and slept.

The children came round him:
Jimmy, Roger, and Jane;
They lifted his head timidly
And let it sink again.

'Look, he's gone sound asleep, Miss,'
Said Jimmy Adair;
'He stays up all the night, you see;
His mother doesn't care.'

'Stand away from him, children.'
Miss Andrews stooped to see.
'Yes, he's asleep; go on
With your writing, and let him be.'

'Now's a good chance!' whispered Jimmy;
And he snatched Bill's pen and hid it.
'Kick him under the desk, hard;
He won't know who did it.'

'Fill all his pockets with rubbish –
Paper, apple-cores, chalk.'
So they plotted, while Jane
Sat wide-eyed at their talk.

Not caring, not hearing,
Bill Craddock he slept on;
Lips parted, eyes closed –
Their cruelty gone.

'Stick him with pins!' muttered Roger.
'Ink down his neck!' said Jim.
But Jane, tearful and foolish,
Wanted to comfort him.

*John Walsh*

**I**

'Winter' by Gareth Owen
'Out of School' by Hal Summers

★ Read both poems, then provide each of the children with a copy to refer to during a re-reading and free ranging discussion immediately following.

★ Initiate a discussion on playground activities before you introduce the poems. (This may work best immediately following a break.) Prompt them, if necessary, to consider activities which vary according to seasons, and to suggest reasons for the differences. Introduce the poems at an appropriate time during the discussion.

★ **i** Read both poems to the whole class then divide into groups of three or four to discuss them. Suggest that they take account of similarities and differences, including the effect of the time of day or the seasons of the year on the pictures the poems give of a playground.

**ii** Give each group the task of compiling a list of the 10 activities most commonly seen in the playground, not necessarily restricted to activities mentioned in the poems.

**iii** Share the final lists amongst the groups. This may lead to further discussion as the activities in their own lists are compared with those in the poems.

**iv** Conclude with a re-reading of the two poems.

**II**

★ 'Four o'clock Friday' by Derek Stuart

**i** Either read the poem yourself or play a prepared tape of a reading. A tape will enable you to observe first reactions to the poem. Don't give out copies at this stage.

**ii** Encourage the class to talk about it. Who are referred to by 'I' and 'they'?

**iii**  If discussion remains tentative, re-read the poem then display it in a prominent position to return to another day.

[A suggested first encounter with 'The Bully Asleep' comes in the course of a development of 'Four o'clock Friday' on page 36.]


## DEVELOPMENTS

'Winter'/'Out of School'

★     **i**  In whatever open space is available – maybe just the classroom with furniture moved to the sides – ask everyone to adopt the position in which they find it easiest to concentrate on what is in their own head without distractions. Once this is done, ask them to picture a Winter or a Summer playground.

[You might talk them through this. See Part II Section 8.]

After building a mental picture of the playground itself, lead them on to imagine the mass of children within it, and finally a single playground activity.

**ii**  Form a sitting circle to exchange details of the pictures they have imagined. Encourage them at this stage to concentrate on the playground and the groups of children rather than the specific activities they were picturing in their heads.

**iii**  Re-read the two playground poems.

**iv**  Ask each one to find a space. (If you are working in a classroom you will need to prepare for this.) Within the time taken for you to count slowly to five, ask them to express, on the spot, one activity that they were picturing, through movements and, possibly, sound. Suggest that they may find it helpful to represent the activity in slow motion.

**v**  Freeze the action. Ask some individuals to show what they have produced, and to talk or answer questions about their activity and the movements and sound they have chosen to represent it.

**vi**  Return to individual work on activities. They may now reject original ideas in favour of others, or may re-work and polish their initial attempt.

**vii**  When all appear to be ready introduce inter-action by encouraging them to continue but also to respond to the activities of others.

**viii**  Gather the class together and discuss playground activities which involve both co-operation and non-co-operation such as arguments, fights, teasing . . .

**ix**  Conclude with pre-arranged readings – volunteered and prepared – of the two playground poems.

★  **i**  Re-read 'Winter', after giving out copies of the poem. Invite discussion of any words, lines or passages in the poem they feel are particularly significant.

**ii**  Divide into small groups to prepare a way of conveying through action their interpretation of the lines:

> And the cold is an ache in the blood
> And a pain on the tender skin
> Beneath finger nails.

**iii**  Look at the resulting action from volunteering groups and make comments.

**iv**  Divide the class into two. Give one of the playground poems to each group and explain the task: to build up a tableau of one of the playground scenes taken from their poem and to prepare a reading of the poem to accompany the viewing of the tableau by an audience. They should try to capture not only the visual picture but also the mood. Everyone should be involved in either the tableau or the reading.

**v**  Give each half of the class the opportunity to view the other half's finished work. Conclude this by inviting the audience to question/discuss the likely feelings of individual characters within the tableau. At this stage the tableau characters may speak for themselves.

★  [Throughout this session you might agree not to name any known bullies or victims.]

**i**  Re-read 'Four o'clock Friday' after checking that everyone has a copy of the poem.

**ii**  As a whole class or in groups make lists of words or phrases that describe the 'I' and 'they' of the poem.
(These lists may include contradictory words: some children may see the 'I' as weak yet consider 'they' to include some attractive figures – from fiction or from real life.)

**iii**  Make the lists available for casual discussion and further thought before another session, or move on to **iv**.

35

**iv** Suggest that a possible way of learning more about a bully might be to interview him, or her. This can be done using a combination of role play and hot-seating. (See Part II Sections 13 and 14.) If you decide to hot-seat a role-played bully it may be prudent and most productive to interview more than one person at a time. One format would be to hot-seat three 'bullies', one boy, one girl and an available adult, providing that they are all first able to familiarise themselves with the poem. Mixing the sexes is important, if only to explore any differences between girl and boy bullies. Bringing in an adult will free you to contribute as one of the questioners and to be aware of children's individual responses. This may suggest your future focus.

**v** When the interview has run its course, or if working in role proves to be so emotive that you need to defuse the situation, draw the hot-seating to a close and read 'The Bully Asleep'. Follow this with a class discussion leading to the similarities and differences between the content of the two poems and the way they are written. What reason could there be for thinking that the second poem shows a more complicated view of bullying than the first?

**vi** Conclude with a further reading of the poems.


## FURTHER DEVELOPMENTS

★ Make use of the earlier work on tableaux to accompany readings of the poems by groups or individuals. You might share these with other classes.

★ Prepare a tape of playground sounds to accompany a tableau and/or a reading.

★ Build up a frieze depicting a playground scene. Display words, phrases or extracts from the poems alongside. The thoughts of children depicted in the frieze might be added by using 'thought bubbles'.

★ Using either a diary or a story format write about how the 'I' or 'they' from 'Four o'clock Friday' spend their weekend.

★ Either individually or in pairs, write a poem with a similar format to Derek Stuart's, but cataloguing the week of one of the bullies. (Remember that a bully may also be bullied elsewhere.)

★ Make a collection of poems on the subject of a playground. Share all the poems selected by reading and display. These could be made into a class anthology available amongst whatever other poetry books are at hand.

★     **i**   Encourage children to write their own playground poems.

     **ii**   Mount a display of their own poems, perhaps amongst other school poems that they have heard or found.


## RELATED POEMS

'The Classroom' – John Mole *The Mad Parrot's Countdown* Peterloo Poets.
'Early bird does catch the fattest worm' – John Agard *Say It Again, Granny* Bodley Head.
'Teacher said . . .' – Judith Nicholls *Magic Mirror and Other Poems* Faber.
'Friends' – Gareth Owen *Salford Road* Young Lions.
'Tables' – Valerie Bloom in *Poetry Jump-Up* (comp. Grace Nichols) Puffin.
'Another Day' – John Cunliffe *Standing on a Strawberry* Deutsch.
'Rodge said' – Michael Rosen *You Tell Me* Puffin.
'Nooligan' – Roger McGough *You Tell Me* Puffin.
'Timothy Winters' – Charles Causley *Collected Poems 1951–75* Macmillan.

listen to one or two retellings

Charles Causley lives in Launceston, in Cornwall, where he was born more than 70 years ago. He decided before leaving school that he wanted more than anything to be a writer:

> *I always wanted to write a book. I loved reading from the time when I was a tiny boy . . . I knew that I would rather meet somebody who'd written a book than meet the King or the Pope or the Tzar of Russia. . . . It seemed to me a wonderful kind of magical trick to be able to do it.*

My earliest memory of reading a Causley poem to a class goes back to the 1960s. That was 'Nursery Rhyme of Innocence and Experience' from the first collection he published. I have included his poems increasingly in poetry sessions with all ages since then. They have the sharpness of vision and perception associated with the finest poetry. They bring words and music into a dynamic fusion that is recognisably his own.

He is widely regarded as one of the major poets of our time. Roger McGough, known to many teachers through his own poetry, has said that if he were allowed to keep the work of only three living poets, Charles Causley would be his first choice.

## BY ST THOMAS WATER

By St Thomas Water
Where the river is thin
We looked for a jam-jar
To catch the quick fish in.
Through St Thomas Churchyard
Jessie and I ran
The day we took the jam-pot
Off the dead man.

On the scuffed tombstone
The grey flowers fell,
Cracked was the water,
Silent the shell.
The snake for an emblem
Swirled on the slab,
Across the beach of sky the sun
Crawled like a crab.

'If we walk,' said Jessie,
'Seven times round,
We shall hear a dead man
Speaking underground.'
Round the stone we danced, we sang
Watched the sun drop,
Laid our heads and listened
At the tomb-top.

Soft as the thunder
At the storm's start
I heard a voice as clear as blood,
Strong as the heart.
But what words were spoken
I can never say,
I shut my fingers round my head,
Drove them away.

'What are those letters, Jessie,
Cut so sharp and trim
All round this holy stone
With earth up to the brim?'
Jessie traced the letters
Black as coffin-lead.
*'He is not dead but sleeping,'*
Slowly she said.

I looked at Jessie,
Jessie looked at me,
And our eyes in wonder
Grew wide as the sea.
Past the green and bending stones
We fled hand in hand,
Silent through the tongues of grass
To the river strand.

By the creaking cypress
We moved as soft as smoke
For fear all the people
Underneath awoke.
Over all the sleepers
We darted light as snow
In case they opened up their eyes,
Called us from below.

Many a day has faltered
Into many a year
Since the dead awoke and spoke
And we would not hear.
Waiting in the cold grass
Under a crinkled bough,
Quiet stone, cautious stone,
What do you tell me now?

## DICK LANDER

When we were children at the National School
We passed each day, clipped to the corner of
Old Sion Street, Dick Lander, six foot four,
Playing a game of trains with match-boxes.

He poked them with a silver-headed cane
In the seven kinds of daily weather God
Granted the Cornish. Wore a rusted suit.
It dangled off him like he was a tree.

My friend Sid Bull, six months my senior, and
A world authority on medicine,
Explained to me just what was wrong with Dick.
'Shell-shopped,' he said, 'You catch it in the war.'

We never went too close to Dick in case
It spread like measles. 'Shell-shopped, ain't you, Dick?'
The brass-voiced Sid would bawl. Dick never spoke.
Carried on shunting as if we weren't there.

My Auntie said before he went away
Dick was a master cricketer. Could run
As fast as light. Was the town joker. Had
Every girl after him. Was spoiled quite out

Of recognition, and at twenty-one
Looked set to take the family business on
(Builders' merchants, seed, wool, manure and corn).
'He's never done a day's work since they sent

Him home after the Somme,' my Uncle grinned.
'If he's mazed as brush, my name's Lord George.
Why worry if the money's coming in?'
At firework time we throw a few at Dick.

Shout, 'Here comes Kaiser Bill!' Dick stares us through
As if we're glass. We yell, 'What did you do
In the Great War?' And skid into the dark.
'Choo, choo,' says Dick. 'Choo, choo, choo, choo, choo, choo.'

## RILEY

Down in the water-meadows Riley
Spread his wash on the bramble-thorn,
Sat, one foot in the moving water,
Bare as the day that he was born.

Candid was his curling whisker,
Brown his body as an old tree-limb,
Blue his eye as the jay above him
Watching him watch the minjies swim.          *(minnows)*

Four stout sticks for walls had Riley,
His roof was a rusty piece of tin,
As snug in the lew of a Cornish hedgerow
He watched the seasons out and in.

He paid no rates, he paid no taxes,
His lamp was the moon hung in the tree.
Though many an ache and pain had Riley
He envied neither you nor me.

Many a friend from bushes or burrow
To Riley's hand would run or fly,
And soft he'd sing and sweet he'd whistle
Whatever the weather in the sky.

Till one winter's morning Riley
From the meadow vanished clean.
Gone was the rusty tin, the timber,
As if old Riley had never been.

What strange secret had old Riley?
Where did he come from? Where did he go?
Why was his heart as light as summer?
*'Never know now,' said the jay. 'Never know.'*

## MAGGIE DOOLEY

Old Maggie Dooley
Twice a day
Comes to the Park
To search for the stray,
Milk in a bowl,
Scraps on a tray,
'Breakfast time!' 'Supper time!'
Hear her say.

Alone on a bench
She'll sit and wait
Till out of the bushes
They hesitate:
Tommy No-Tail
And Sammy No-Fur,
Half-Eye Sally
And Emmy No-Purr.

She sits by the children's
Roundabout
And takes a sip
From a bottle of stout.
She smiles a smile
And nods her head
Until her little
Family's fed.

Whatever the weather,
Shine or rain,
She comes at eight
And eight again.
'It's a Saint you are,'
To Maggie I said,
But she smiled a smile
And shook her head.

'Tom and Sammy,
Sally and Em,
They need me
And I need them.
I need them
And they need me.
That's all there is,'
She said, said she.

## THE MONEY CAME IN, CAME IN

My son Sam was a banjo man,
His brother played the spoons,
Willey Waley played the ukelele
And his sister sang the tunes:
     Sometimes sharp,
     Sometimes flat,
     It blew the top
     Off your Sunday hat,
     But no one bothered
     At a thing like that,
     And the money came in,
       came in.

Gussie Green played a tambourine,
His wife played the mandolin,
Tommy Liddell played a one-string fiddle
He made from a biscuit tin.
>Sometimes flat,
>Sometimes sharp,
>The noise was enough
>To break your heart,
>But nobody thought
>To cavil or carp,
>And the money came in,
>>came in.

Clicketty Jones she played the bones,
Her husband the kettle drum,
Timothy Tout blew the inside out
Of a brass euphonium.
>Sometimes sharp,
>Sometimes flat,
>It sounded like somebody
>Killing the cat,
>But no one bothered
>At a thing like that,
>And the money came in,
>>came in.

Samuel Shute he played the flute,
His sister played the fife.
The Reverend Moon played a double bassoon
With the help of his lady wife.
>Sometimes flat,
>Sometimes sharp
>As a pancake
>Or an apple tart,
>But everyone, everyone
>Played a part
>And the money came in,
>>came in.

## FIRST ENCOUNTERS

★    Spend some time during the week before you intend to focus on these poems building up anticipation:

> Pin up a copy of one of the five poems daily, possibly grouped together, possibly scattered.
> Don't do more than encourage everyone to read them, possibly not even that.
> Aim to heighten curiosity.
> Avoid naming the author.
> Avoid making any comment on connections there are between the poems.

In the course of the week you might let it be seen that you are preparing readings of each of the poems with volunteers from the class. (Some of the poems may be better read by more than one voice. See Part II Section 3.)

★    **i**  Introduce all the poems in a single session using prepared readings by different voices or groups of voices, live or recorded.

    **ii**  Either give out copies of the poems or prepare overheads for the class to follow as each poem is re-read.

★    [Spread over more than one session]

    **i**  Talk about churchyards:
— any they know of?
— any they have visited frequently?
— any personal churchyard experiences to tell?

    **ii**  Introduce 'By St Thomas Water' as a story which centres on a churchyard. Read it aloud.

    **iii**  Give out copies and allow time for the class to re-read it.

    **iv**  Set up groups for re-telling the story *within each group* – each group member trying to tell the next stage in correct sequence, the others in the group assisting when necessary.

    **v**  Listen as a class to one or two-re-tellings by groups or individuals.

    **vi**  Discuss the poem as a story. Were there things that they particularly liked or disliked about the way it was 'told'?

**vii**   Go on to treat one or more of the following poems: 'Riley', 'Maggie Dooley' and 'Dick Lander' in the same way, in each case focussing on the poem *as story*. Keep 'The Money Came in, Came in' until last.

**viii**   Prepare a reading of 'The Money Came in, Came in' which makes full play of the rhythm and the sounds. [If you enjoy music and can find someone who sings there is a fine musical setting in the hardback edition of *Early in the Morning*. The class could soon pick up the tune.] Invite the groups to discuss this as a story.

**ix**   Draw the class together and extend the discussion to as many of this group of Causley poems as they have read. This discussion may touch on:
—   what they expect from a story
—   beginnings, middles, ends
—   the part played by shape/pattern/repetition/rhyme/rhythm
—   characters/relationships/conflicts/voices

Follow where the pupils lead, particularly in the early stages of the discussion, without putting ideas into their heads.


## DEVELOPMENTS


★   Divide the class into groups of 4–6. Assign *one* of the Charles Causley poems to each group. Ask them to choose one of the following ways of dealing with their poem:

**A**   Prepare a taped reading taking account of the atmosphere/mood of the poem.
—   What might you do through sound *before*, *during* and *after* the reading to create effects which will help to draw listeners in?
—   How might different voices or combinations of voices help the impact of the reading?

**B**   Prepare a live reading of the poem using however many voices you need, whilst the others in the group mime or create tableaux. Bear in mind what might be done *before*, *during* and *after* the reading, when the voices are silent, to add to the listeners' experience of the poem.

**C**   Prepare a version of the poem which depends on accompanying movement. The movement should:
—   focus attention on the words for those watching, not distract them.
—   heighten awareness of any changes that occur in the poem.

★     Divide the class into five groups. Allocate a different poem to each group. They have two tasks:

**A**  *Preparing a section of 'A Causley Frieze',* based on
 (i)  the characters in their poem, or
 (ii)  incidents in their poem, or
 (iii)  both.
  [Because all of the class is involved in this it requires some preliminary decisions/instructions, such as:
  —  a minimum and a maximum number of pictures required from each group
  —  an agreed size for each picture
  —  colours to be used.]
The finished pictures will make a substantial frieze around the classroom or along one wall.
  Include Charles Causley's name and the titles of the poems prominently within the display. (Associating the names of poets with familiar poems or collections in the Poetry Book Box or on the classroom shelf is part of the *bringing poetry alive* process.)

**B**  *Preparing their contribution to 'A Causley Concert'*
Each group prepares a reading of their allocated poem involving them all in some way, together with appropriate sound. The reading must be true to the *sense* and the *feeling* and the *spirit* of the words. When all the groups are ready put the readings together as a live concert, possibly for a school assembly or for another class, and/or recorded for other classes to hear. (Two classes – maybe in different schools – might prepare tapes to exchange and compare.)

## FURTHER DEVELOPMENTS

★       **i**  Draw attention to the differences of mood in these poems. Some are funny, some sad, some magical, some mysterious, but in each case the poet has consciously created the mood by the *words* used and the *pictures* put into the reader's or the listener's head. For example, I read the poem 'Riley' as a celebration of a mysterious, enchanting and contented being. It does not enter my head that something terrible has happened *to* Riley by the end of the poem because that would be inconsistent with the mood that has been created. Now if I want to defend these statements I can only do it by referring to *words* and *pictures* within the poem that create the *mood*: for example, the words 'snug' and 'he envied neither you nor me', and the pictures suggested by

Many a friend from bushes or burrow
To Riley's hand would run or fly,

And soft he'd sing and sweet he'd whistle
Whatever the weather in the sky.

**ii** Encourage any who feel confident to take a subject of their own choice and to write either a story or a poem in which they attempt to create a distinct mood.

**iii** Ask any who prefer a precisely defined structure to write down on a scrap of paper:
   **a** a place (an old house; a railway-station; a super-modern, fully-automated flat; a river bank . . .);
   **b** a person, and a little bit of information about that person (an old man; a visitor who doesn't speak the local language; a young woman in a great hurry . . .);
   **c** a mood (funny, sad, mysterious . . .).

When this is done exchange papers.
   Each should then try to write a story or a poem about the place and person they have been given, and create the suggested mood.

**RELATED POEMS from Charles Causley's most recent work:**

'Mawgan Porth', 'Why' and 'Serena' in *Jack the Treacle Eater* Macmillan

'One for the Man', 'There Was an Old Woman' and 'When I Was a Boy' in *Early in the Morning* Puffin

'Buffalo', 'This Clock' and 'Sunday School Outing' in *A Field of Vision* Macmillan

**For teachers:**
*Talking with Charles Causley* – Brian Merrick – NATE
A primary teacher in Cornwall for more than twenty years, Causley talks with humour and illumination about how he taught poetry. The book is full of helpful ideas. It includes a short biography of the poet and a selected booklist of the collections most useful for a teacher. (Available from NATE Publications at the address given in Part III.)

SECTION 5

recording observations
around the poem

Anyone browsing in a bookshop, reading a survey of poetry books currently in print (such as the splendid *Poetry 0–16*: see page 134) or simply referring to the booklists in Part III of this volume must be struck by the range of poetry that is available: the range of voices and the range of places and times and experiences that have formed them.

Poems invite contrast. In an earlier book, *Exploring Poetry: 5–8*, Jan Balaam and I contrasted two versions of an old and widely known ballad which reflected how different people in different times and places had reshaped an old story and told it with a new voice. One of the versions had 8 × 4 line verses. The other had 7 × 7 line verses. Another ballad, 'Sir Patrick Spens', similarly exists in many versions and perhaps the *most* striking thing about them is the difference in the length. The shortest and the best – but also the most challenging textually – is included in *A Book of Old Ballads*, edited by Beverley Nichols, splendidly illustrated by H. M. Brock, and published in 1934. It is based on an old manuscript copy from Scotland and tells the story in eleven verses. Another version of the same ballad appears in *The Rattlebag* in 14 verses, and yet another in the *Oxford Book of Poetry for Children* in 22 verses.[1] Contrasting can be a lively and rewarding activity. It is also an interesting way of exploring what makes a poem. This section focusses on two contrasting pairs.

The first pair are both about cats. One is by Edward Brathwaite. He was born in Barbados and teaches at the University of the West Indies. He has spent a lot of time in the U.K. and has frequently given powerful readings of his poetry, some on television. He founded the Caribbean Artists Movement here and has written plays for children.

The second is by Stevie Smith, who was born in 1903, in Hull. She moved to London when she was three years old and lived there for the rest of her life. She wrote novels and poetry and became widely known through her entertaining and frequently startling readings and broadcasts. She died in 1971. Many people may know her best through *Stevie*, the play by Hugh Whitemore, which has been widely performed and has also been televised, with Glenda Jackson in the title role.

The second pair of poems for contrast share the same title, 'Fairy Tale'. The first is by Miroslav Holub, who was born in Czechoslovakia in 1923. He is regarded as Czechoslovakia's outstanding poet and, in the judgement of Ted Hughes and many others, is 'one of the half dozen most important poets writing anywhere'. His poem, like those of Nika Turbina, is mediated for us by the additional voice of a translator.

The second poem in this pair is by Katherine Mansfield. She was born in New Zealand in 1888 and died in 1923, the year that Holub was born. She is best known as a writer of short stories and much of her poetry, like the example included here, has a quaint, but pleasing, 'period' flavour. Since I believe that many children would enjoy that flavour I have included a new collection, published in 1988, in one of the lists in Part III.

1.  For details of both books see page 59.

## CAT

To plan plan to create to have
whiskers cool carat silver ready and curved
bristling

to plan plan to create to have
eyes green doors that dilate greenest
pouncers

to be ready rubber ball ready
feet bouncers cool fluid in
tension

to be steady steady claws all
attention to wait wait and create
pouncing

to be a cat eeling through alleys
slipping through windows of odours
to feel swiftness slowly

to halt at the gate hearing
unlocking whispers paper feet wrapping
potatoes and papers

to hear nicely mice spider feet
scratching great horny nails
catching a fire flies wire legs etch-

ing yet stretching beyond this arch
untriumphant lazily rubb-
ing the soft fur of home

*Edward Kamau Brathwaite*

## THE SINGING CAT

It was a little captive cat
    Upon a crowded train
His mistress takes him from his box
    To ease his fretful pain.

She holds him tight upon her knee
    The graceful animal
And all the people look at him
    He is so beautiful.

But oh he pricks and oh he prods
    And turns upon her knee
Then lifteth up his innocent voice
    In plaintive melody.

He lifteth up his innocent voice
    He lifteth up, he singeth
And to each human countenance
    A smile of grace he bringeth.

He lifteth up his innocent paw
    Upon her breast he clingeth
And everybody cries, Behold
    The cat, the cat that singeth.

He lifteth up his innocent voice
    He lifteth up, he singeth
And all the people warm themselves
    In the love his beauty bringeth.

*Stevie Smith*

*FAIRY TALE*

He built himself a house,
    his foundations,
    his stones,
    his walls,
    his roof overhead,
    his chimney and smoke,
    his view from the window.

He made himself a garden,
    his fence,
    his thyme,
    his earthworm,
    his evening dew.

He cut out his bit of sky above.

And he wrapped the garden in the sky
and the house in the garden
and packed the lot in a handkerchief

and went off
lone as an arctic fox
through the cold
unending
rain
into the world.

*Miroslav Holub*
*Translated by Ian Milner*
*and George Theiner*


*FAIRY TALE*

Now folds the Tree of Day its perfect flowers,
And every bloom becomes a bud again,
Shut and sealed up against the golden showers
Of bees that hover in the velvet hours . . .
    Now a strain
Wild and mournful blown from shadow towers,
Echoed from shadow ships upon the foam,
Proclaims the Queen of Night.
    From their bowers
The dark Princesses fluttering, wing their flight
To their old Mother, in her huge old home.

*Katherine Mansfield*

# FIRST ENCOUNTERS

**I** 'Cat' and 'The Singing Cat'

★ Prepare an acetate sheet for an overhead projector showing the complete poem 'Cat', and another showing 'The Singing Cat'.

    **i**  **a** Read either of the two poems aloud to the class before showing it, and allow time for initial jotted reactions leading to full class comments on the poem which they have so far only heard.

      **b** Project the poem on a screen or wall and ask for silent reading.

      **c** Read it aloud again while the class follows.

      **d** Invite observations about any patterns they can see or hear, repetitions, words that seem specially important (including the title) or anything they find striking about the poem. Using a variety of coloured felt tips record their observations around the poem on the acetate sheet.

(This is another activity not to be rushed. Keep your notes on the sheet *very simple* and use colours consistently: for example,
— one colour underlining for *rhymes*
— another for *repetitions*
— another for *striking words or phrases*
— arrows, loops and circles for connections or patterns
— any words used kept to a minimum.
Non-permanent markers allow you to make alterations and to use the same sheet repeatedly.)

      **e** Conclude with another reading and further reactions and comments, taking account of the different readings they have heard and the notes so far made on the projected copy of the poem.

    **ii** (Probably at a separate session.)
Follow the same sequence as in **i**, but based on the second of the two poems. This time, when you come to stage **d**, you might distribute copies for pupils to record their own observations, working in pairs or in threes. Draw attention to the strategies that you used, including colours, signs and underlinings.

★     **i** Introduce each poem to the class as one poet's treatment of a closely linked theme. You might begin with a few words about the poet based on the facts provided in the introduction to this section.

**ii** Follow this by asking for silent readings of both poems.

**iii** Invite reactions and comments. If any of the following do not arise spontaneously, you might introduce them as direct questions:
— which of the two poems did you find easier to take in at a first reading?
— what is it about the cat in each poem that seems most to interest the poet?
— do you find any difficulties about thinking of the cat in each of these poems as the same 'animal'?

**II** 'Fairy Tale'

★ **i** Introduce the term 'fairy tale' as a topic for discussion, beginning in small groups then opening it up to the whole class. Suggest that they include in their discussions:
— what they expect from a fairy tale
— what happens in a fairy tale
— what sort of people or events such tales contain.

**ii** Read each of the 'Fairy Tale' poems to the class. Allow time after each reading for any instant comments but at this stage delay prolonged discussion.

**iii** Equip everyone in the class with a piece of paper, preferably A3 size, for sketching. Repeat your reading of each poem *possibly two or three times* with extended gaps in between while each individually makes one or more rough sketches based on the words of the poem.

**iv** Share the results in small groups before considering, as a full class, which poem gave stronger prompts for pictures.

**v** Return to the common title, 'Fairy Tale', and to their earlier statements about the expectations it arouses. What is in each poem that makes the title appropriate?

★ Use the same sequence of activities based on a projected copy of each poem suggested for 'Cat' and 'The Singing Cat'.

## DEVELOPMENTS

★ **i** Work in pairs or small groups. Distribute a sheet of paper to each group, preferably A3 size. Choosing either pair of poems ask them to:

56

a) Head the sheet with the titles of the two poems and the names of the writers.

b) Divide the remainder of the sheet into two columns.

c) Head one column *SIMILARITIES*, the other *DIFFERENCES*.

**ii** Ask them to examine the two poems carefully, listing any detail that strikes them under each heading.

[With the two versions of 'Fairy Tale', for example, they might list the title under *Similarities*.

Under *Differences* they might list the pattern and shape given to the poem in the Miroslav Holub version by –

'He built . . .'
'He made . . .'
'He cut out . . .'
'And he wrapped . . .'
'and packed . . .'
'and went off . . .'

and the pattern and shape given to the poem in the Katherine Mansfield version by –

'the Tree of Day'
'the Queen of Night'
and 'the dark Princesses'.

With 'Cat' and 'The Singing Cat' they might note under *Similarities* the fact that both poems make use of rhyme and repetition.

Under *Differences* they might note that 'The Singing Cat' uses rhyme very regularly at the end of the 2nd and 4th lines but 'Cat' uses it very irregularly, as with 'create' (lines 1, 4, 11), 'dilate' (line 5), 'wait' (twice in line 11), 'gate' (line 16), 'potatoes' (line 18).]

**iii** When all groups are ready ask for a representative from each to read their lists. Build up a composite list on the board as each new similarity or difference is reported.

**iv** Conclude with a re-reading of each poem by you or a volunteer from the class.

★ **i** Consider the poems within either pair specifically from the viewpoint of language. Look at:

**a** the poet's *choice* of words
**b** the poet's *grouping* of words.

Is there anything surprising, pleasing, difficult, strange?

**ii** Working in twos or threes ask them:

**a** to list examples where the *choice* or the *grouping* of words strongly affects the sound or rhythm of the poem.

**b** to find at least one example where the choice or the grouping adds something to the poem in addition to meaning, sound or rhythm.

[You might consider, as examples:
  'rubber ball ready' – 'Cat'
  'lifteth', 'singeth' – 'The Singing Cat'
  'his chimney and smoke' – 'Fairy Tale' (Holub)
  'the golden showers' – 'Fairy Tale' (Mansfield).]

**iii** Invite suggestions about connections there might be between the way words are used in the poem and the effect *the writer wants the poem to have on the reader* (to amuse, to create a mood or atmosphere, to capture the 'essence' of the subject matter, to tell a story . . .)
Pursue this as long as interest lasts and encourage precise examples to support suggestions made.

**iv** Working in groups ask them to plan a presentation for *one* of the poems intended to project particularly the qualities they consider most important in the language of the poem and what they imagine is the effect the poet intended it to have on its readers or audience. (See Part II Sections 3 and 10.)

## FURTHER DEVELOPMENTS

★ Divide the class into groups to prepare a reading of 'Cat'. They should focus particularly on:
  — the *flow* of the words
    (where is it appropriate to pause?)
  — the *pace*
    (where fast, where slow?)
  — *stress* or *emphasis*
    (words? sounds? rhymes?)
  — rhythm.

Allow ample time for preparing this reading before listening – as a full class – to *all* of the groups.
Give time to *contrasting* one reading with others, and talking about the differences.

[This might all take place within one session or be spread over a sequence of sessions. If recorded the readings might be kept as part of a growing collection of class/school made tapes.]

★ Individually or in pairs ask the class to prepare a re-telling – written or spoken – of 'The Singing Cat' or either version of 'Fairy Tale'.
Make time for listening to all of these – read aloud or told – and for discussion about which of the poems lent itself best to being treated in this way.
You might proceed to consider what was gained and what was lost in each re-telling, and whether you might have included 'Cat' for treatment in this way.

★ Invite the class, working individually and possibly over an extended period of time, to use any of these poems as a model – in terms of subject, *and/or* shape, *and/or* line, verse or section patterns – on which to write a poem of their own.

★ Discuss with a musical member of staff the possibilities of linking any or all of these poems with music: available on record or improvised. 'Cat' – in particular – also lends itself to exploration/appreciation through movement.

★ All four poems lend themselves to posters combining the full text of the poem and illustration. These make an effective medium for expressing personal or group experience of a poem. (See Part II Section 17.)

[By still treating the poems in pairs, double posters could effectively express the *contrast* between the poems experienced by the group in a combined verbal and visual form.]


## *RELATED POEMS FOR CONTRAST*


'The Song of Wandering Aengus' – W. B. Yeats in *Oxford Book of Poetry for Children* (ed. Edward Blishen) O.U.P.
'The Forlorn Sea' – Stevie Smith *Selected Poems* Penguin.

'who knows if the moon's' – e. e. cummings *Selected Poems 1923–58* Faber.
'Moonlit Apples' – John Drinkwater in *Golden Apples* (ed. Fiona Waters) Piper Books.

'Mister Fox' – Anon and 'A Fox Jumped Up One Winter's Night' – Anon in Jan Balaam and Brian Merrick *Exploring Poetry: 5–8* NATE.

'Sir Patrick Spens' – Anon in *The Rattlebag* (ed. Seamus Heaney and Ted Hughes) Faber.
'Sir Patrick Spens' – Anon in *Oxford Book of Poetry for Children* (ed. Edward Blishen) O.U.P.

ask them to create a still picture . . .

Christine Hall writes:

The poems chosen in this section were used with children in the upper juniors. These children were used to the pleasures derived from reading poetry; it had become part of their normal reading diet. In this situation the teacher needs to be particularly discerning. There has to be scope for extending appreciation and understanding, and for the challenge of new formats and ideas.

The easily accessible poem may therefore not be the most suitable choice. For all four poems I used drama as a means of exploration. Drama offers a development of children's appreciation through physical as well as mental involvement. The nature of this involvement leads to increased understanding. Through the medium of drama children can first give shape to their experience of the poem and subsequently reflect upon it.

The four poems have the common themes of social relationships, power, guilt and responsibility, but they also have individual areas of concern and a variety of presentation. Despite these differences all four provide a succinct view of the world around us. Through their exploration of such poems children may become better acquainted with their own world and more able to interpet, understand and cope with it.

'This Letter's To Say' and 'Old Johnny Armstrong' provide an obvious progression. 'Old Johnny Armstrong' can be viewed as the possible result of the types of decision-making evident in the first poem. It provides a sharp focus for what might happen to the recipient of the letter in 'This Letter's To Say'. Its tone however is very different. It is more personal and individually focussed, therefore requiring a different form of exploration.

'A Case of Murder' explores darker areas of responsibility and guilt through the relationship between a child who has been left alone by his parents in a basement flat and a cat which he hates. The horrific consequences have a psychological aspect not explored in the first two poems.

'New Members Welcome' is an example of the power and economy of poetry. It provides a contrast in style to the first three poems, whilst sharing many of their fundamental themes.

All these poems offer interesting and exciting possibilities for further exploration across the full range of expressive arts. Although drama is proposed as the main form through which children explore them initially, the work suggested also draws on and contributes to the other arts.

*THIS LETTER'S TO SAY*

Dear Sir or Madam,
This letter's to say
Your property
Stands bang in the way
Of Progress, and
Will be knocked down
On March the third
At half-past one.

There is no appeal,
Since the National Need
Depends on more
And still more Speed,
And this, in turn,
Dear Sir or Madam,
Depends on half England
Being tar-macadam.
(But your house will —
We are pleased to say —
Be the fastest lane
Of the Motorway.)

Meanwhile the Borough
Corporation
Offer you new
Accommodation
Three miles away
On the thirteenth floor
(Flat Number Q
6824).

But please take note,
The Council regret:
No dog, cat, bird
Or other pet;
No noise permitted,
No singing in the bath
(For permits to drink
Or smoke or laugh
Apply on Form
Z 327);
No children admitted
Aged under eleven;
No hawkers, tramps
Or roof-top lunches;
No opening doors
To Bible-punchers.

Failure to pay
Your rent, when due,
Will lead to our
Evicting you.
The Council demand
That you consent
To the terms above
When you pay your rent.

Meanwhile we hope
You will feel free
To consult us
Should there prove to be
The slightest case
Of difficulty.

With kind regards,
Yours faithfully . . .

*Raymond Wilson*

## OLD JOHNNY ARMSTRONG

Old Johnny Armstrong's eighty or more
And he humps like a question-mark
Over two gnarled sticks as he shuffles and picks
His slow way to Benwell Park.

He's lived in Benwell his whole life long
And remembers how street-lights came,
And how once on a time they laid a tram-line,
Then years later dug up the same!

Now he's got to take a lift to his flat,
Up where the tall winds blow
Round a Council Block that rears like a rock
From seas of swirled traffic below.

Old Johnny Armstrong lives out his life
In his cell on the seventeenth floor,
And it's seldom a neighbour will do him a favour
Or anyone knock at his door.

With his poor hands knotted with rheumatism
And his poor back doubled in pain,
Why, day after day, should he pick his slow way
To Benwell Park yet again? —

O the wind in park trees is the self-same wind
That first blew on a village child
When life freshly unfurled in a green, lost world
And his straight limbs ran wild.

*Raymond Wilson*


## A CASE OF MURDER

They should not have left him there alone,
Alone that is except for the cat.
He was only nine, not old enough
To be left alone in a basement flat,
Alone, that is, except for the cat.

64

A dog would have been a different thing,
A big gruff dog with slashing jaws,
But a cat with round eyes mad as gold,
Plump as a cushion with tucked-in paws —
Better have left him with a fair-sized rat!
But what they did was leave him with a cat.
He hated that cat; he watched it sit,
A buzzing machine of soft black stuff,
He sat and watched and he hated it,
Snug in its fur, hot blood in a muff,
And its mad gold stare and the way it sat
Crooning dark warmth: he loathed all that,
So he took Daddy's stick and he hit the cat.
Then quick as a sudden crack in glass
It hissed, black flash, to a hiding place
In the dust and dark beneath the couch,
And he followed the grin on his new-made face,
A wide-eyed, frightened snarl of a grin,
And he took the stick and he thrust it in,
Hard and quick in the furry dark,
The black fur squealed and he felt his skin
Prickle with sparks of dry delight.
Then the cat again came into sight,
Shot for the door that wasn't quite shut,
But the boy, quick too, slammed fast the door:
The cat, half-through, was cracked like a nut
And the soft black thud was dumped on the floor.
Then the boy was suddenly terrified
And he bit his knuckles and cried and cried;
But he had to do something with the dead thing there.
His eyes squeezed beads of salty prayer
But the wound of fear gaped wide and raw;
He dared not touch the thing with his hands
So he fetched a spade and shovelled it
And dumped the load of heavy fur
In the spidery cupboard and its hot low purr
Grows slowly louder year by year:
There'll not be a corner for the boy to hide
When the cupboard swells and all sides split
And the huge black cat pads out of it.

*Vernon Scannell*

## NEW MEMBERS WELCOME

Pull the blinds on your emotions
Switch off your face.
Put your love into neutral.
This way to the human race.

*Spike Milligan*

## FIRST ENCOUNTER

★   ·   **i** Give every child a large sheet of paper and a felt pen. Read the poems out aloud and after each poem ask the children to brainstorm any ideas, emotions, reactions which have occurred during the reading. It is important to emphasise that the aim is to get ideas down quickly. Accuracy of spelling is not important at this stage, and repetitions may well occur.

**ii** After reading all four poems in this way ask the children in small groups to share what they have written, looking out for linking or contrasting themes, common features between the poems and similarities between their observations. These can then be shared with the whole class.

**iii** Give each child a copy of the poems and allow time for silent reading. The four poems may then be read aloud by children within their group.

**iv** Still within the small groups, return to the earlier brainstormed sheets. Are there any additions or alterations to be made now? Share these with the whole class.

**v** Working again as a full class, draw on the small group impressions to build up an overview of the children's reactions to the four poems. Using the board or one large sheet of drawing paper for the whole class map out specific areas of agreement and note any disagreements. Make it clear there are no right or wrong answers. From this initial gathering of ideas, collectively focus on more specific questions:
— can you outline the story, if any, of each poem?
— to what extent are we invited to speculate, and about what?
— how are we left feeling at the end of each poem?
— are there any words or lines in each poem which shape how we feel?
Try also to steer the children from believing their task is to explain the *meaning* of the poem and concentrate rather on the variety of responses within the class and the areas of agreement and disagreement, for further exploration.

## DEVELOPMENTS

'This Letter's To Say'

★    **i** After a brief discussion of the poem, ask the children in pairs to take on the role of the house owner and the person responsible for sending the letter. Explain that you want them to devise a scene in which the two meet after the letter has been written. Allow the children time to develop the drama: if rushed they may not engage with the meaning, and may lose the opportunity to discover the irony evident in the poem.

ii    Allow the pairs to show their scenes to the full group and at the end of the individual pieces introduce the device of 'Hot-Seating'. (See Part II Section 14.) This will allow the rest of the children to ask each pair questions about the scene, and the two children to answer in role. This lessens the likelihood of superficial responses and involves the whole class in every interpretation.

'Old Johnny Armstrong'

★    i    Use Role Play (see Part II Section 13) to develop the character of Johnny Armstrong. This will draw the children into the poem. The person in role could be a teacher, a pupil or another adult familiar with this method of working. Some possible aids for moving into role are:

a    the use of a prop, such as the gnarled sticks, or of a particular body posture, as a signal to the children that a role change has taken place.

b    a bag or bundle of clothes or props explored and speculated upon by the whole group, and with their help gradually accepted by the person going into role as the old man. In this way the children are instrumental in creating the character. This is particularly useful when a child goes into role.

c    the use of changing tone and posture in the course of reading the poem which indicates to the children that the reader is taking on the role of the old man. This can be further emphasised by putting a direct question to the children from Johnny Armstrong on finishing the reading.

[By taking on an appropriate role, such as a Social Worker or a relative of Johnny, the teacher can encourage the children to ask the old man questions. These questions should be quite closely related to information gained from the poem which gives a genuine reason for close scrutiny of the poem. It may also give the opportunity to make connections between this poem and the first.]

ii    When an overall picture of the man's life has been created, specific areas of the poem can be examined. The last verse is important for the understanding of the poem as a whole. In groups ask the children to discuss the contrast between the life of the child and that of the old man, choosing words from the last verse which indicate these differences.

**iii** Keeping the same groups ask them to express some aspect of the poem in a short improvisation.

'A Case of Murder'

★     **i** In groups of three give the children time to read and discuss the poem. From here ask them to create a still picture of a scene which for them captures the essence of the poem. (See Part II Section 12.) The choice of three in the group gives the children the possibility of using one as 'director' in building up the still picture or allows them to attempt to represent the cat. It is important to emphasise that they do not have to create a literal representation of a particular moment in the poem. Nor will the still pictures have to develop into an improvisation.

**ii** Provide opportunity for the children to show their still pictures. Encourage the audience to speculate, paying particular attention to the structure of the 'stills': how is information gleaned about relationships from body language, eye contact, etc.? From here the children can individually 'hot-seat' any of the characters within the still picture. By this means the children take control through the process of genuine questioning and answering.

**iii** If they have not taken account of the end of the poem move on to a second still picture task. This should focus solely on the last five lines. By narrowing the focus in this way and becoming less concerned with the linear, story-telling structure of the poem deeper meanings can be revealed.

'New Members Welcome'

★     **i** After an unhurried re-reading of the poem ask the children in small groups to discuss how the three previous poems illuminate these four lines, and conversely how this poem relates to each of the others.

**ii** Through full class discussion share these opinions with the whole class, possibly building a list of connections on the board.

**iii** By means of tableaux (see Part II Section 12) try to illustrate or express some of the metaphors used in the poem, such as 'pull the blinds on your emotions', 'switch off your face' . . . This necessitates group discussion on the nature, meaning and use of metaphors, possibly extended to metaphors beyond those included in the poem.

69

[If possible photograph the tableaux, preferably in black and white, for use in the 'photographic' Further Development. (See page 71). Take two photographs of each, the second of the tableau draped with a cloth or other covering.]

## FURTHER DEVELOPMENTS

'This Letter's To Say'

★ Organise a full-scale campaign of protest within the community, using a teacher or another volunteer in role and including letters of protest and complaint. This could be backed by campaign posters, and the design of alternative, more acceptable housing estates or motorway routes.

'Old Johnny Armstrong'

★ Use dance and music to explore the contrasts evident in this poem. Work on differences in the movements of old and young and those associated with ideas such as freedom, restriction and powerlessness. Emphasis can be placed on aspects of stillness, silence, and variations in speed and levels, culminating in a sequence which explores the use of space and sound to express the contrasts.

'A Case of Murder'

★ **i** Make masks which encapsulate the qualities of the 'creature' growing in the cupboard. The children should be encouraged to explore how masks transform the wearer, and to avoid making literal representations of the cat. (See Part II Section 19.)

**ii** Write either a piece of prose or poetry related to their mask: how it transforms them, what it is like visually, people's responses to it . . .

'New Members Welcome'

★ Using the idea of the human race as a 'club', devise a list of requirements needed for membership. This can be for an imagined 'Utopian' world, or how the children perceive it to be now.

70

★ Use the photographs taken during stage **iii** of the Development of 'New Members Welcome' as the basis for drawings on form, texture, shape and tone.

★ Use the brainstormed sheets produced during the First Encounter (see page 67) as the basis for personal writing – of any kind: stories, poems, newspaper reports, interviews . . .


## RELATED POEMS

'I am' – Chun Po Man, and 'Ballad of Sixty-Five' – Alma Norman in *I Like That Stuff* (ed. Morag Styles) C.U.P.

'Tall Story' – Geoffrey Summerfield *Welcome, and other poems* Deutsch.

'An Old Woman of the Roads' – Padraic Colum in *Golden Apples* (ed. Fiona Waters) Piper.

'Lie' – Nika Turbina *First Draft* Marion Boyars.

*provide wax crayons, chalks,*
*pastels . . . for a poster*

Nika Turbina was born in 1974 and still lives in Yalta, U.S.S.R. She is a celebrated poet in Russia where we are told poetry enjoys something of the popularity that football does in Britain! An L.P. of her readings sold over 30,000 copies there and she received enthusiastic receptions when she read her poems in Europe and the U.S.A.

The collection from which these poems are taken is called *First Draft*. After being published in the U.S.S.R. when she was ten years old it was published in Italy – where it won the Golden Lion of Venice prize – and in France. It is now available in the U.K. and can be ordered through any bookseller.[1]

The poet Yevtushenko, in his introduction to the collection, comments on the suggestion that Nika Turbina is unlike any other eight-year-old:

> *This book makes one think that children in general perceive the world in a much more adult way than we think. But not all children know how to express that and Nika does.*

I first became aware of the poems through a review in *The Guardian* by the poet Carol Ann Duffy. The following are extracts from that review:

> *A young child does not have the complex layers of experience of an adult, but she has experience of, and is still experiencing, childhood – a state which adults have forgotten, or only half remember . . .*

> *Reading this book, we can look, uncomfortably, on our own adult failures and see, in a poet's truthfulness, the fears we have bequeathed to our children. This is their voice, wherever they live:*
> > *My day is so small*
> > *and I want kindness*
> > *so much*
> > *for everyone*

When I read the collection I was curious about the effect the poems might have on children of the writer's age. My guess was that many would like them and be intrigued by an eight-year-old's international success. I believed that they might also be stirred by the force, the feeling, the honesty, and the clarity of the poems and could be roused to respond to them – not only in words but through a variety of forms and media.

I put together the two small groups of Nika's poems given here and some suggestions about how they might be introduced in a classroom. I then asked some teachers particularly interested in teaching poetry to try them. The work on which this section is based was carried out with 8–11 year olds.

One of the teachers, who had read them with a class of 9–10 year olds, reported afterwards:

*I think the children responded enthusiastically to the poems and enjoyed the ideas put forward. Some are difficult but as with anything like this there are layers of meaning, and these could well be the kind of poems that children will return to later to peel off another layer and discover further delights. They certainly are challenging, and I think the children responded to these challenges with enjoyment, even if they didn't overcome the difficulties. Several of them wanted to take the poems away to keep.*

1.   Published by Marion Boyars Ltd. £6.95.

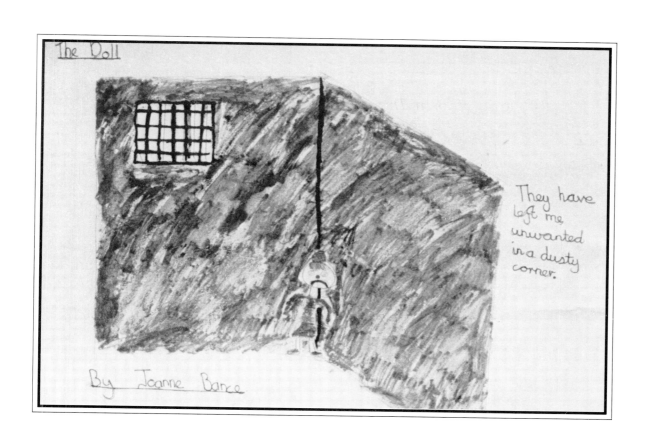

## THE VOICE

Down the parkway
like a crystal ball
your ringing voice
passed me.

It ran along rooftops,
it ran along leaves,
in the autumnal rustle
it captured music.

Suddenly, it stopped
near the bench,
with the smashed
lamp post.

Your crystal ball
sparkled with laughter.
And the smashed lamp post
suddenly glowed light.

## I WANT KINDNESS

How often
I catch sidelong glances
and sharp words hurt me
like arrows
I implore you – listen! You must not
destroy the shortlived
childlike dreams in me.
My day is so small,
and I want kindness
so much
for everyone
even those
who aim
at me.

## DON'T LISTEN TO LAMP POSTS

Don't listen to lamp posts.
They send you to sleep.
Put aside sorrow.
The time will come
when sadness and ill luck will cease
and the stars will call you to them.
Don't listen to lamp posts.
They send you to sleep.

## I'LL BE LOST IN THE FOG

I'll be lost in the fog
like a tiny star
in the sky.
I'll be lost in the fog
and no one
cares about me.
But I go forward,
because I believe in my path.
It will definitely
bring me to the sea.
All paths meet there,
the bitter ones
and the ones easy to follow.
And I will give the sea my star,
which I carry carefully
in my hands.
That is my future,
but it is so big . . .
It's hard
to carry it alone.

## THE DOLL

I am like a broken doll.
They forgot to put a heart in my chest.
They have left me, unwanted
in a dusty corner.
But just before morning
I hear a quiet whisper:
'Sleep, my dear
for a long time, years
will pass,
and when you wake up
people will want to
pick you up again
they will cuddle you and play with you
and then your heart will beat.'
But it's frightening to wait for that.

## FIRST ENCOUNTERS

★ Use the information in the introduction to this section to arouse class interest in Nika Turbina before they see or hear the poems.
[You may equally well decide to keep this until they have encountered the poems with an open mind.]

★ **i** Prepare readings of the first group of poems.
Let the class hear them once or twice without the words in front of them and then again, with. If they seem interested, allow time for further silent reading.

**ii** Display all the poems read on the classroom wall and encourage individuals or pairs to prepare their own readings of one that appeals. Provide opportunity for the preparation and an audience for the readings.

★ After a time for free and independent response, but while interest is still high, provide opportunity for informal group talk about the poems. If necessary suggest some focusses for comment:
— what experiences does Nika Turbina write about?
— what activities?
— what objects?
— what scenes?
— how does she express feeling in the poems?
— are there some feelings that she writes about in more than one poem?
— what connection is there between the poems and the titles?
— is the connection always the same?

You might introduce these as random non-sequential questions around the display of poems after the display has been up for a while, without implying that you expect anyone to provide formal answers.

★ When you feel the moment is right to expand what you have been doing, introduce the second group of poems by Nika Turbina. You might repeat the previous procedure or cut any part that you feel was unsuccessful before or would not bear repeating.

## DEVELOPMENTS

★ Divide the class into groups of 6–8, each group to prepare a reading of the poems and a brief introduction to be presented to:

**i** the other groups.

78

**ii** an audience who has not heard the poems before: other classes, an assembly, a parent-teacher meeting, etc.

★ Suggest/provide materials for collages, paintings, posters to accompany the display of poems.

★ Encourage written responses or reactions to the poems in a variety of forms:
— poems
— letters
— stories
— imagined dialogues
— personal anecdotes recalled by the poems
— imagined dialogue with the poet
— a sequence of questions, addressed to the poet.
These might be added to the existing display of poems or form an additional display.

## FURTHER DEVELOPMENTS

★ Provide wax crayons, chalks, pastels, pencils, paint for a poster which includes quotations from a single poem or a theme/image which runs through several poems (isolation, hope, lamp-posts, stars . . .)

★ Make a word collage against an appropriate background relating to a single poem, or a linking pair/group.

## RELATED POEMS

*SOME COLLECTIONS OF POETRY WRITTEN BY CHILDREN:*

*Bossy Parrot* – Best Poems from *The Evening Chronicle* Poetry Competition – Bloodaxe Books

*The Earthsick Astronaut* – Selected Poems from *The Observer* National Children's Poetry Competition – Puffin.

*Cadbury's Book of Children's Poetry* (eighth in an annual series) – Beaver

*Young Words* – Poems and stories from the W.H. Smith annual Young Writers' Competition, 1990 – W.H. Smith

*Check with your L.E.A. about local collections of children's poetry that may be available.*

*aim at a forceful
and energetic delivery*

Sound is an element in all poems, but in some it is central. These are really performance-poems needing at the very least dramatic reading. This section offers four poems which make different use of sound. 'Posting Letters' uses sound to create atmosphere and mood in the telling of a vivid childhood experience. 'The Tin Can Band' uses sound to create a scene rich in noise, colour and movement: a poem which needs to be read aloud, ideally by many voices, with other accompanying sounds. The same might be said about 'Sensemaya: A Chant for Killing a Snake', in which the poetry is linked to human activity: the sense of deadly purpose and the participating group contribute to the poem's hypnotic power.[1]

The fourth poem is probably the best known. It draws on a wide range of shapes, patterns and devices associated with sound to tell an ancient story: the testing of Daniel in the lions' den. It is a sparkling set-piece for performance and presentation.

The suggestions in this section have been applied to a variety of poems, all included in the list of *Related Poems* at the end of this section. But these four are chosen for their contrast. The prominence of the sound and its impact on the reader is different in each one and invites different classroom approaches.

The poems as a group might form a single unit or be spread out over an extended period.

1.   *Note*   A recording by John Agard is available on one of two cassettes of Caribbean Poetry available from Harcourt Brace Jovanovich Ltd. (See page 134.) Originally for ILEA Learning Materials Service it is part of a collection of recorded poems compiled by Lorna Cocking and Joan Goody.

## POSTING LETTERS

There are no lamps in our village,
And when the owl-and-bat black night
Creeps up low fields
And sidles along the manor walls
I walk quickly.

It is winter;
The letters patter from my hand
Into the tin box in the cottage wall;
The gate taps behind me,
And the road in the sliver of moonlight
Gleams greasily
Where the tractors have stood.

I have to go under the spread fingers of the trees
Under the dark windows of the old man's house,
Where the panes in peeling frames
Flash like spectacles
As I tip-toe.
But there is no sound of him in his one room
In the Queen-Anne shell,
Behind the shutters.

I run past the gates,
Their iron feet gaitered with grass,
Into the church porch,
Perhaps for sanctuary,
Standing, hand on the cold door ring,
While above
The tongue-tip of the clock
Clops
Against the hard palate of the tower.

The door groans as I push
And
Dare myself to dash
Along the flagstones to the great brass bird,
To put one shrinking hand
Upon the gritty lid
Of Black Tom's tomb.

Don't tempt whatever spirits stir
In this damp corner,
But
Race down the aisle,
Blunder past font,
Fumble the door,
Leap steps,
Clang iron gate,
And patter through the short-cut muddy lane.

Oh, what a pumping of breath
And choking throat
For three letters.
And now there are the cattle
Stirring in the straw
So close
I can hear their soft muzzling and coughs;
And there are the bungalows,
And the steel-blue miming of the little screen;
And the familiar rattle of the latch,
And our own knocker
Clicking like an old friend;
And
I am home.

*Gregory Harrison*

## THE TIN CAN BAND

Oh, the tin can band,
Oh, the tin can band!
It's the dinniest band
In the big bright land.
It's a sing-song band, it's a bing-bong band.
It's a miss-a-beat, have-a-treat, skippy-feet band,
As we march along with our pots and pans,
And we bing and bong on our old tin cans.

We're a-singing and a-songing to the binging and the bonging.
We're escaping and a-skipping out
On every hand.

And it sounds like a battle
When our tin cans rattle,
When our tin cans rattle
And our tin cans clang.
Yes, it's sounding like the prattle and the tattle of a battle
Like a merry monster cannon going
BANG, BANG, BANG!

Though silence falls when the band's gone by,
And the street is bare to the hills and sky,
There's a nitter and a natter,
And a tiny tinny patter,
Like a whisper (only crisper)
Like a tin toy's sigh,
And a flutter like a mutter,
Like a sunny sort of stutter,
Going giggling down the gutter
Where the funny echoes die.

*Margaret Mahy*

### SENSEMAYA: A CHANT FOR KILLING A SNAKE

Mayombe-bombe-mayombe!
Mayombe-bombe-mayombe!
Mayombe-bombe-mayombe!

The snake has eyes of glass;
the snake comes and coils itself round a pole;
with his eyes of glass, round a pole,
with his eyes of glass.
The snake walks without legs;
the snake hides in the grass;
walking he hides in the grass
walking without legs.

Mayombe-bombe-mayombe!
Mayombe-bombe-mayombe!
Mayombe-bombe-mayombe!

If you hit him with an axe he will die.
Hit him hard!
Do not hit him with your foot, he will bite,
do not hit him with your foot, he is going away!

Sensemaya, the snake,
Sensemaya.
Sensemaya, with his eyes,
Sensemaya.
Sensemaya, with his tongue,
Sensemaya.
Sensemaya, with his mouth,
Sensemaya —

Dead snake cannot eat;
dead snake cannot hiss;
cannot walk,
cannot run.
Dead snake cannot look;
dead snake cannot drink,
cannot breathe,
cannot bite.

Mayombe-bombe-mayombe!
Sensemaya, the snake —
Mayombe-bombe-mayombe!
Sensemaya, it is still —
Mayombe-bombe-mayombe!
Sensemaya, the snake —
Mayombe-bombe-mayombe!
Sensemaya, it is dead.

*Nicolas Guillen*
Translated by G. R. Coulthard

## THE DANIEL JAZZ

Darius the Mede was a king and a wonder.
His eye was proud, and his voice was thunder.
He kept bad lions in a monstrous den.
He fed up the lions on Christian men.

Daniel was the chief hired man of the land.
He stirred up the music in the palace band.
He whitewashed the cellar. He shovelled in the coal.
And Daniel kept-a-praying:– 'Lord save my soul.'
Daniel kept-a-praying:– 'Lord save my soul.'
Daniel kept-a-praying:– 'Lord save my soul.'

Daniel was the butler, swagger and swell.
He ran up stairs. He answered the bell.
And *he* would let in whoever came a-calling:–
Saints so holy, scamps so appalling.
'Old man Ahab leaves his card.
Elisha and the bears are a-waiting in the yard.
Here comes Pharaoh and his snakes a-calling.
Here comes Cain and his wife a-calling.
Shadrach, Meshach and Abednego for tea.
Here comes Jonah and the whale,
And the *Sea*!
Here comes St Peter and his fishing pole.
Here comes Judas and his silver a-calling.
Here comes old Beelzebub a-calling.'
And Daniel kept a-praying:– 'Lord save my soul.'
Daniel kept-a-praying:– 'Lord save my soul.'
Daniel kept-a-praying:– 'Lord save my soul.'

His sweetheart and his mother were Christian and meek.
They washed and ironed for Darius every week.
One Thursday he met them at the door:–
Paid them as usual, but acted sore.
He said:– 'Your Daniel is a dead little pigeon.
He's a good hard worker, but he talks religion.'
And he showed them Daniel in the lion's cage.
Daniel standing quietly, the lions in a rage.
His good old mother cried:–
'Lord save him.'
And Daniel's tender sweetheart cried:–
'Lord save him.'

And she was a golden lily in the dew.
And she was as sweet as an apple on the tree.
And she was as fine as a melon in the corn-field.
Gliding and lovely as a ship on the sea,
Gliding and lovely as a ship on the sea.

And she prayed to the Lord:—
'Send Gabriel. Send Gabriel.'

King Darius said to the lions:—
'Bite Daniel. Bite Daniel.
Bite him. Bite him. Bite him!'

Thus roared the lions:—
'We want Daniel, Daniel, Daniel,
We want Daniel, Daniel, Daniel.
Grrrrrrrrrrrrrrrrrrrrrrrrrrrrrrrr
Grrrrrrrrrrrrrrrrrrrrrrrrrrrrrrrrr.'

And Daniel did not frown.
Daniel did not cry.
He kept on looking at the sky.
And the Lord said to Gabriel:—
'Go chain the lions down,
Go chain the lions down,
Go chain the lions down,
Go chain the lions down.'

And Gabriel chained the lions,
And Gabriel chained the lions,
And Gabriel chained the lions.
And Daniel got out of the den,
And Daniel got out of the den,
And Daniel got out of the den.
And Darius said:— 'You're a Christian child.'
Darius said:— 'You're a Christian child.'
Darius said:— 'You're a Christian child.'
And gave him his job again,
And gave him his job again,
And gave him his job again.

*Vachel Lindsay*

## FIRST ENCOUNTERS

★    Arrange the first encounter with the poems as a group in a way that will provide the maximum level of aural impact and enjoyment of the sounds and rhythms. You might arrange for different readers and different methods of presentation.

Allow time for some general discussion at the end about striking impressions; memorable lines, words or subsections; and similarities or contrasts between or within the poems.

★    Introduce each poem separately, possibly on quite different occasions, but in each case as you progress establish connections with those already looked at and invite discussion about the contrasting importance of sound.

## DEVELOPMENTS

'Posting Letters'

★    **i** As a class discuss different kinds of fear:
— are there situations that *everyone* is afraid of?
— is fear always unpleasant?
— is there a difference between the fear of going to the dentist, for example, and the fear of the dark?

**ii** Read, or re-read, the poem. If the class has heard it before you might give the option of reading it silently or aloud with a partner.

**iii** Continue the class discussion, but now relate it to the poem:
— in what way(s) does the poem deal with fear?
— is there more than one kind here?
— what evidence is there to suggest that the person in the poem (boy? girl?) deliberately encourages the fright she/he experiences?

**iv** Divide the class into groups of 3 or 4, with an agreed note-keeper. Their task is in four parts:
     **a** Make two lists. In the first list all of the words in the poem that are to do with *movement*. In the second all of the words that are to do with *sound*. Sometimes they may need to list more than one word as in 'walk quickly' or 'I have to go'.
     **b** Plan a sequence of six sounds to accompany a reading of the poem. In selecting the sounds they should choose those that will

90

most powerfully create atmosphere for the listeners, such as 'pumping of breath'.

c Work on a group reading to which the whole group should contribute. (Point out the possible value of having more than one voice for some lines or sections.)

d Combine the sounds with the reading either in a live performance for the rest of the class or in a recording for them to listen to. (Inviting another class – or more – to join the audience for the readings can increase the challenge of the task and the quality of the preparation and consequently heighten the likelihood of close engagement with the poem.)


'The Tin Can Band' or 'Sensemaya'

★　　i Read the poem to the class. Aim at a forceful and energetic reading, strongly stressing contrasts of sounds, volume and pace.

ii Distribute copies of the poem and allow time for individual reading.

iii Discuss your reading of it:
— was it easy to listen to?
— did it bring out the real qualities of rhythm and sound offered by the poem?
— can they suggest other ways of reading it?
— are there any words that they don't understand?

iv Concentrate on reading the opening 10–12 lines. Divide the class into groups of 3 or 4 to decide on good readings, possibly taking it 2/3 lines at a time. Circulate while this is happening, like a director wanting to arrive at a good reading of the whole verse – rehearsed and polished.

v Listen to some of the polished readings and afterwards discuss what was good and bad about them. What other things might they have done?

vi Each group now prepares a reading or full-scale presentation of the whole poem for all the other groups. Set a time limit – say, 25–30 minutes – at the end of which they are all to be ready for performing. If possible, arrange different corners in the school where groups can work without distraction.
[An alternative, if enough cassette players and spaces are available, is to ask for finished recordings instead of live presentations, all of which you listen to at the end of the set time.]

'The Daniel Jazz'

★ Prepare a presentation of the poem that will involve everyone in the class.

This could range from a simple and static choral reading to an elaborate dramatised performance involving considerable preparation. Whichever appeals to you most, one starting point for the preparation might be an annotated script on which you have marked (maybe in collaboration with some children) changes of speaker and your production notes for the rehearsals.

In the first working session all members of the class will need blank copies of the poem on which they can mark, with your direction, all the lines they will be speaking and any other directions relating to them personally. Highlighters are ideal for this activity.

For those who have not attempted work of this kind before, the following pages show scripts prepared in two ways: the first script is marked with notes for one possible production of the poem involving movement, mime, dramatisation, tableaux and mask-making, the second with notes for one possible choral reading. When looking at these it is important to remember that *any one pupil will see a clean copy of the poem on which to mark only personally relevant lines and instructions.*

## *FURTHER DEVELOPMENTS*

★      **i** Look at the way the writer in 'Posting Letters' uses sound. In the lines

         And when the owl-and-bat black night
         Creeps up low fields
         And sidles along the manor walls
         I walk quickly

the sounds themselves are sinister, quite apart from the picture they are painting. 'Creeps' and 'sidles' both *sound* threatening, even if you don't know what they mean. (It's not easy to *creep* or *sidle* in a friendly way.)

The sense of creeping is helped by the slow and drawn out 'ee' sound (compare it with the short, sharp 'a' in bat, for instance) and this 'ee' sound is then echoed in 'fields'. There is another slow and drawn out sound in this line in 'low', so that 'Creeps up low fields' actually *sounds* slow.

What about the 's' sounds in this line, and in the next?

Any comments about the sound in

         **a** 'owl-and-bat black'
         **b** 'owl' and 'low'
         **c** 'walls' and 'walk'?

     **ii** Set the class to write individually about some time when they did something . . .

  **a** to frighten themselves
  **b** to test their own nerve
  **c** to frighten someone else.
Suggest that they consciously attempt to create atmosphere in the way they write about it, bearing in mind the techniques used by Gregory Harrison in 'Posting Letters'.

★ Examine some of the ways the writers are using and creating sound in the other poems.

★ Another poem by Margaret Mahy is called 'Clowns'. It begins:

> Zing! goes the cymbal. Bang! goes the drum.
> See how they tipple-topple-tumbling come.

Ask the class, singly or in pairs, to continue the poem in their own way, keeping in mind that it is intended for reading aloud.

★ Divide the class into small groups. Present them with the choice of four or five poems which lend themselves to performance or choral readings (see *Related Poems*) from which they can choose one on which to make notes for a group reading or performance.

## RELATED POEMS

'Cat' – see Section 5.
'The Money Came In, Came In' – see Section 4.
'The Building Site' – Gareth Owen *Song of the City* Young Lions.
'The Chant of the Awakening Bulldozers' – Patricia Hubbell in *Junior Voices I* (ed. Geoffrey Summerfield) Penguin.
'Ping-Pong' – Gareth Owen *Salford Road* Young Lions.
'Poetry Jump Up' and 'Woodpecker' – John Agard in *I Like That Stuff* (ed. Morag Styles) C.U.P.
'Richard's Brother Speaks' – Desmond Strachan, and 'Fisherman's Chant' – John Agard in *You'll Love This Stuff* (ed. Morag Styles) C.U.P.
'Woodpecker' – Ted Hughes *Under the North Star* Faber.
'Smith's Song' – George Sigerson, and 'Poem from a Three-Year-Old' – Brendan Kennelly in *Irish Poems* (ed. Bridie Quinn and Seamus Cashman) Wolfhound Press.
'Tailor' – Eleanor Farjeon in *A Puffin Quartet of Poets* (ed. Eleanor Farjeon) Puffin.

Use the natural pauses in the poem to re-arrange the stage-setting.

Stage area initially bare. Actors sitting off-stage come forward as referred to.

Cast
Storyteller (S)
King Darius (D)
Daniel (Dan)
Gabriel (G)
Mother (M)
Sweetheart (Sw)
Lions (L)
4 Groups of voices

## THE DANIEL JAZZ

Gp1 Darius the Mede was a king and a wonder.
Gp2 His eye was proud, and his voice was thunder.
Gp3 He kept bad lions in a monstrous den.
Gp4 He fed up the lions on Christian men.

Gp1 Daniel was the chief hired man of the land.
Gp2 He stirred up the music in the palace band.
Gp3/Gp4 He whitewashed the cellar. He shovelled in the coal.
Gp1/D And Daniel kept-a-praying:— 'Lord save my soul.'
Gps 1+2/D Daniel kept-a-praying:— 'Lord save my soul.'
All Gps + D Daniel kept-a-praying:— 'Lord save my soul.'

S Daniel was the butler, swagger and swell.
He ran up stairs. He answered the bell.
And *he* would let in whoever came a-calling:—
Saints so holy, scamps so appalling.
Gp1 'Old man Ahab leaves his card.
Gp4 Elisha and the bears are a-waiting in the yard.
Gp2 Here comes Pharaoh and his snakes a-calling.
Gp3 Here comes Cain and his wife a-calling.
Gps 1+2 Shadrach, Meshach and Abednego for tea.
Gps 3+4 Here comes Jonah and the whale,
All Gps And the *Sea*!
Gp1 Here comes St Peter and his fishing pole.
Gp2 Here comes Judas and his silver a-calling.
Gps 3+4 Here comes old Beelzebub a-calling.'
S/Dan And Daniel kept a-praying:— 'Lord save my soul.'
Gps 3+4/Dan Daniel kept a-praying:— 'Lord save my soul.'
All Gps/All + Dan Daniel kept a-praying:— 'Lord save my soul.'

↑ all the movement in this section is Daniel's ↓

S His sweetheart and his mother were Christian and meek.
They washed and ironed for Darius every week.
One Thursday he met them at the door:—
Paid them as usual, but acted sore.
/D He said:— 'Your Daniel is a dead little pigeon.
He's a good hard worker, but he talks religion.'
S And he showed them Daniel in the lion's cage.
Gps 1+2/Gps 3+4 Daniel standing quietly, the lions in a rage.
Gps 1+2 His good old mother cried:—
M 'Lord save him.'
Gps 3+4 And Daniel's tender sweetheart cried:—
Sw 'Lord save him.'

↑ action + emotion ↓

Props + Costumes
Shawls for mother + sweetheart
Halo? Wings? for angel
Crown for King
Lion face masks

94

| | |
|---|---|
| M | And she was a golden lily in the dew. |
| S | And she was as sweet as an apple on the tree. |
| Gps 1+2 | And she was as fine as a melon in the corn-field. |
| S | Gliding and lovely as a ship on the sea, |
| All voices | Gliding and lovely as a ship on the sea. |

*lyrical*

| | |
|---|---|
| M | And she prayed to the Lord:– |
| Srv | 'Send Gabriel. Send Gabriel.' |

*(intense)*

| | |
|---|---|
| S | King Darius said to the lions:– |
| D/D+S | 'Bite Daniel. Bite Daniel. |
| D,S+Gps 1+2/D,S+ Gps 3+4/ All voices | Bite him. Bite him. Bite him!' |

| | |
|---|---|
| S | Thus roared the lions:– |
| L | 'We want Daniel, Daniel, Daniel, |
| All voices, increasing in volume and ferocity | We want Daniel, Daniel, Daniel. |
| | Grrrrrrrrrrrrrrrrrrrrrrrrrrrrrrrr |
| | Grrrrrrrrrrrrrrrrrrrrrrrrrrrrrrrrr.' |

| | |
|---|---|
| (rising) Sw | And Daniel did not frown. |
| ( " ) M | Daniel did not cry. |
| M+Sw | He kept on looking at the sky. |
| S | And the Lord said to Gabriel:– |
| S+Gps 1+2 | 'Go chain the lions down, |
| S+Gps 3+4 | Go chain the lions down, |
| S + AllGps | Go chain the lions down, |
| All voices | Go chain the lions down.' |

*stately + solemn*

| | |
|---|---|
| Sw | And Gabriel chained the lions, |
| M | And Gabriel chained the lions, |
| Sw, M+S | And Gabriel chained the lions. |
| G | And Daniel got out of the den, |
| D | And Daniel got out of the den, |
| All voices | And Daniel got out of the den. |
| S/D | And Darius said:– 'You're a Christian child.' |
| S+D, M+Sw | Darius said:– 'You're a Christian child.' |
| All Gps | Darius said:– 'You're a Christian child.' |
| Dan | And gave him his job again, |
| All except groups | And gave him his job again, |
| All voices | And gave him his job again. |

*Vachel Lindsay*

Basic Set

*increasing action*

95

Notes for a Choral Reading. (i) Divide the class into two roughly equal groups. From each group select two solo readers and also cast the following parts: Daniel, Darius, Mother, Sweetheart.
(ii) Consider the positioning of the groups. Would it be appropriate to begin and end with a tableau? Are the soloists to speak from within the group? Do you want movement at any point?

## THE DANIEL JAZZ

Gp 1 { Darius the Mede was a king and a wonder.
{ His eye was proud, and his voice was thunder.
Gp 2 { He kept bad lions in a monstrous den.
{ He fed up the lions on Christian men.

S1   Daniel was the chief hired man of the land.
S2   He stirred up the music in the palace band.
S3/S4  He whitewashed the cellar. He shovelled in the coal.
Gp 1  And Daniel kept-a-praying:– 'Lord save my soul.'
Gp 2  Daniel kept-a-praying:– 'Lord save my soul.'
Gps 1+2/D  Daniel kept-a-praying:– 'Lord save my soul.'

S1   Daniel was the butler, swagger and swell.
S2/S3  He ran up stairs. He answered the bell.
Gp 1 { And *he* would let in whoever came a-calling:–
{ Saints so holy, scamps so appalling.
S1   'Old man Ahab leaves his card.
S2   Elisha and the bears are a-waiting in the yard.
S3   Here comes Pharaoh and his snakes a-calling.
S4   Here comes Cain and his wife a-calling.
Gp 1  Shadrach, Meshach and Abednego for tea.
Gp2  Here comes Jonah and the whale,
Gps 1+2  And the *Sea*!
S1   Here comes St Peter and his fishing pole.
S2   Here comes Judas and his silver a-calling.
S3   Here comes old Beelzebub a-calling.'
Gp1+D  And Daniel kept a-praying:– 'Lord save my soul.'
Gp2+D  Daniel kept-a-praying:– 'Lord save my soul.'
Gps1+2/D  Daniel kept-a-praying:– 'Lord save my soul.'

S1   His sweetheart and his mother were Christian and meek.
S2   They washed and ironed for Darius every week.
S3   One Thursday he met them at the door:–
S4   Paid them as usual, but acted sore.
/Dar  He said:– 'Your Daniel is a dead little pigeon.
He's a good hard worker, but he talks religion.'
Gp1  And he showed them Daniel in the lion's cage.
Gp2  Daniel standing quietly, the lions in a rage.
Gps 1+2  His good old mother cried:–
M   'Lord save him.'
Gps 1+2  And Daniel's tender sweetheart cried:–
Sw   'Lord save him.'

| | |
|---|---|
| S1 | And she was a golden lily in the dew. |
| S2 | And she was as sweet as an apple on the tree. |
| S3 | And she was as fine as a melon in the corn-field. |
| S4 | Gliding and lovely as a ship on the sea, |
| S1,2,3+4 | Gliding and lovely as a ship on the sea. |

| | |
|---|---|
| M | And she prayed to the Lord:— |
| Sw | 'Send Gabriel. Send Gabriel.' |

| | |
|---|---|
| Gp1 | King Darius said to the lions:— |
| Dar | 'Bite Daniel. Bite Daniel. |
| All | Bite him. Bite him. Bite him!' |

| | |
|---|---|
| S1 | Thus roared the lions:— |
| Gp1 | 'We want Daniel, Daniel, Daniel, |
| Gp2 | We want Daniel, Daniel, Daniel. |
| All | { Grrrrrrrrrrrrrrrrrrrrrrrrrrrrrr |
| | Grrrrrrrrrrrrrrrrrrrrrrrrrrrrrrr.' |

| | |
|---|---|
| S2 | And Daniel did not frown. |
| S3 | Daniel did not cry. |
| S4 | He kept on looking at the sky. |
| S1,2,3+4 | And the Lord said to Gabriel:— |
| All | 'Go chain the lions down, |
| G1 | Go chain the lions down, |
| G2 | Go chain the lions down, |
| S1 | Go chain the lions down.' |

| | |
|---|---|
| S2 | And Gabriel chained the lions, |
| Gp1 | And Gabriel chained the lions, |
| Gp2 | And Gabriel chained the lions. |
| All | And Daniel got out of the den, |
| Gp1 | And Daniel got out of the den, |
| S1 | And Daniel got out of the den. |
| S3/Dar | And Darius said:— 'You're a Christian child.' |
| S4/Gp1 | Darius said:— 'You're a Christian child.' |
| Gp2/Gps1+2 | Darius said:— 'You're a Christian child.' |
| S1,2,3+4 | And gave him his job again, |
| Gps1+2 | And gave him his job again, |
| All | And gave him his job again. |

*Vachel Lindsay*

Additional Effects:
Musical accompaniment?
Masks?
A central throne?
A 'gate' with lion masks
behind?
A Gabriel figure?

*represent the key stages of the poem through four illustrations*

Instinctive judgements about suitable poems are worth testing, particularly with a class which already shows interest and enthusiasm for poetry. This holds true, perhaps especially, even when you are not quite sure what you make of the poem yourself. A poem which intrigues us, which we don't in fact understand, may well be worth exploring with a class for the mutual satisfaction of the exploration itself. A class often helps you to reach a fuller understanding. It also frequently shows you that your earlier response was inadequate, and for the class debunks the notion of poems being puzzles to which the teacher claims to have all the answers.

This section focusses on a pair of poems which produced two absorbed and enthusiastic poetry sessions. The class had developed confidence in the teacher's instincts about what would interest them. This allowed him to risk mistakes. They were 12–13 year olds. Each session lasted a little over an hour. At the end of the two sessions there was little doubt that both poems would be returned to later, and there was a strong likelihood that this would be with repeated satisfaction and increasing perception.

Perhaps not many teachers of classes within the 8–13 range will want to challenge them with the two poems here. But what the poems offer is a stimulating and tested example of how challenging poems may be approached in such a way that there is a good chance of children finding them accessible and, maybe, responding to them with pleasure.

### 'WE ARE GOING TO SEE THE RABBIT . . .'

We are going to see the rabbit,
We are going to see the rabbit.
Which rabbit, people say?
Which rabbit, ask the children?
Which rabbit?
The only rabbit,
The only rabbit in England,
Sitting behind a barbed-wire fence
Under the floodlights, neon lights,
Sodium lights,
Nibbling grass
On the only patch of grass
In England, in England
(Except the grass by the hoardings
Which doesn't count.)
We are going to see the rabbit
And we must be there on time.

First we shall go by escalator,
Then we shall go by underground,
And then we shall go by motorway
And then by helicopterway,
And the last ten yards we shall have to go
On foot.

And now we are going
All the way to see the rabbit,
We are nearly there,
We are longing to see it,
And so is the crowd
Which is here in thousands
With mounted policemen
And big loudspeakers
And bands and banners,
And everyone has come a long way.
But soon we shall see it
Sitting and nibbling
The blades of grass
On the only patch of grass
In – but something has gone wrong!
Why is everyone so angry,
Why is everyone jostling
And slanging and complaining?

The rabbit has gone,
Yes, the rabbit has gone.
He has actually burrowed down into the earth
And made himself a warren, under the earth,
Despite all these people.
And what shall we do?
What *can* we do?

It is all a pity, you must be disappointed,
Go home and do something else for today,
Go home again, go home for today.
For you cannot hear the rabbit, under the earth,
Remarking rather sadly to himself, by himself,
As he rests in his warren, under the earth:
'It won't be long, they are bound to come,
They are bound to come and find me, even here.'

*Alan Brownjohn*

## UNDER A RAMSHACKLE RAINBOW

A dead tree.
On a rotten branch sit two wingless birds. Among leaves
on the ground a man is searching for his hands.
It is fall.

A stagnant marsh.
On a mossy stone sits the man angling. The hook
is stuck in the waterlily.
The waterlily is stuck in the mud.

An overgrown ruin.
In the grass the man sleeps sitting up. A raindrop descends
in slow-motion through space.
Somewhere in the grass a pike flounders.

A dry well.
At the bottom lies a dead fly. In the wood nearby
a spider gropes through the fog.
The man is trapped in the spiderweb on the horizon.

An abandoned ant hill.
Above a little woodmarsh floats the man. The sun
is just going down. The man has already stopped growing.
The ants gather on the shore.

*Ingemar Gustafson*
translated from the Swedish by May Swenson

**I 'We are going to see the rabbit . . .'**

## FIRST ENCOUNTERS

★     Begin in a circle by re-capping on some poems you have recently looked at together. You might re-read one or two to create a receptive mood for encountering a new poem. Read 'We are going to see the rabbit . . .' without giving it a title, and invite first responses. After whatever discussion or comment arises, invite pairs or groups to reach agreement about a suitable title. After hearing their suggestions, and discussing their appropriateness, conclude the session by hearing the poem again.

★     *Stage 1*

    **i**   Establish a mood of concentration, excluding everything but your voice and what is inside the pupils' heads. (See Part II Section 8.)

    **ii**   Talk the class into the future until they are exploring a scene – using all of their senses – say, one hundred years ahead. The pace of this stage should be slow, allowing imaginations to work.

    **iii**   When the class seems ready ask each one to talk to a partner in precise detail about the scene they imagined. What did they see, smell, feel . . . ?

    **iv**   Go on to a full class discussion centring on the similarities and contrasts discovered in the pairs between the imagined scenes.

*Stage 2*

    **i**   Distribute copies of 'We are going to see the rabbit . . .'. Give them the choice of following the words on the page or just listening while you read.

    **ii**   Leave time for them to re-read the poem either to themselves or with a partner.

    **iii**   Invite comments about the future imagined in the poem. They may quite relevantly relate this to the future imagined by themselves. Lead on from this into general discussion about the poem.

    **iv**   Conclude the session with a re-reading of the poem.

## DEVELOPMENTS

★  Work with the full class on a presentation of 'We are going to see the rabbit . . .' using a combination of movement, drama and choral speech. Begin by examining the different voices and viewpoints in the poem: the crowd, the policemen, the loudspeakers, the rabbit . . . and allocating responsibility for these to different groups. In creating the scenes and the mood there may be a lot of improvisation but the poem exactly as written should emerge clearly within the performance.

★  Invite the class, either singly, in pairs or in threes, to work on a collage of the impression made by the poem. For those in a group it must represent an agreed impression. It may convey a single powerful image which captures the whole poem or a sequence of images that tell the story.

★  Provide paper and felt tip pens for each individual to represent the key stages of the poem through four illustrations, using a sheet of paper folded to make four sections. Words or quotations may be included. Allow time for each to show and to talk about the finished work, either in small groups or to the full class. The result could be a wall display built up around a copy of the poem.

## II  Under a Ramshackle Rainbow

## FIRST ENCOUNTERS

★  *Stage 1*

[If you can't use a drama space clear the centre of the classroom.]

  **i**  Ask the pupils to find a space and concentrate on your voice. Focus attention on close sounds – distant sounds – the silence in the room – their own breathing. Stress stillness, silence, concentration. Take time over this.

  **ii**  Divide them into groups of three or four.

  **iii**  Each group must find their own space and then use all three or four bodies to make still photographs. (See Part II Section 12.) Begin with one or two familiar scenes before moving on to calculated leads towards the poem.

[John Seal's sequence was – School at 3.30 – the Houses of Parliament – Fishing beside a Stagnant Pond – the Final Frontier – the JCB as the Solution. He offered no help with any of them. After a lot of consternation, particularly over the last two, all groups managed something. At the end of the 30–40 seconds allowed for deciding what to do with each title he called '1-2-3-Freeze', at which point the photograph had to be complete and still.]

*Stage 2*

    **i**   Each group now use all three or four bodies to make a *sequence* of 3 'still photographs' for each cue that you provide. The cues given should again be relevant to the poem: such as Bleakness or Torment.

[The routine for showing the finished product here needs to establish initial stillness before a further sequence of signals for the change from one 'photograph' to the next. See Part II Section 9.]

    **ii**   If it seems appropriate invite discussion of what they have done so far before introducing the poem.

*Stage 3*

    **i**   Distribute copies of 'Under a Ramshackle Rainbow' and let the class listen to two or three readings made independently by different people, and recorded by you in anticipation of this moment.

    **ii**   If there is time, invite comments on the poem, on the readings and on the connection with what they were doing beforehand.

★    [This could come between Stages 2 and 3 of the previous development or be the sole introduction to Stage 3, above].

    **i**   Choose a piece of music which you feel 'works' in the same way as the poem, and makes a similar demand on the listener.

    **ii**   Request the class to sit wherever they feel most comfortable to listen to the music. Ask them to take note while listening of any still or moving pictures or images that come into their heads.

    **iii**   Allow adequate time for sharing the pictures and images experienced, firstly in small groups, then as a full class. Alert them to a link – in your mind – between the music and the poem.

## DEVELOPMENT

★ *Stage 1*

**i** Form groups of three or four.

**ii** Ask each group to choose one or two sentences from the poem and use all their voices – separately or in chorus – in a reading that matches the poem, however exaggeratedly. Set a time limit – say, 2 minutes.

**iii** Establish a routine to give a brisk play-back – maybe a sequence of groups, each to follow straight on from the previous group.

*Stage 2*

**i** Divide the poem so that all verses are allocated within the groups.

**ii** Each group works out a way of reading their verse *and* a series of movements to go with the reading. Allow plenty of time for this.

**iii** For the play-backs arrange the readings so that all groups not performing can see and hear clearly. Take the verses in sequence and without unnecessary intervals.

**iv** Conclude by re-reading the poem to the class and opening up discussion. Possible starters:
— why do you think the poet wrote this poem?
— is there anything you particularly like or don't like about it?[1]

1. *Note* These were the questions asked. The animated discussion which they produced filled the following twenty minutes of the session, and centred very firmly on the poem, despite the fact that the first is considered, critically, to be 'inadmissable'.

## FURTHER DEVELOPMENTS

★ Build up a spider diagram as you recap on the kind of things already considered about the two poems:

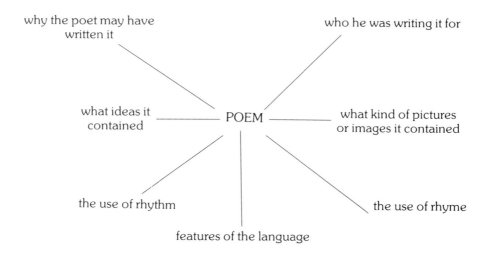

why the poet may have written it

who he was writing it for

what ideas it contained — POEM — what kind of pictures or images it contained

the use of rhythm

the use of rhyme

features of the language

★ Give each member of the class a sheet of paper to divide in the way shown. Ask each of them – working individually or in a group – to list all of the similarities and differences noticed between the two poems.

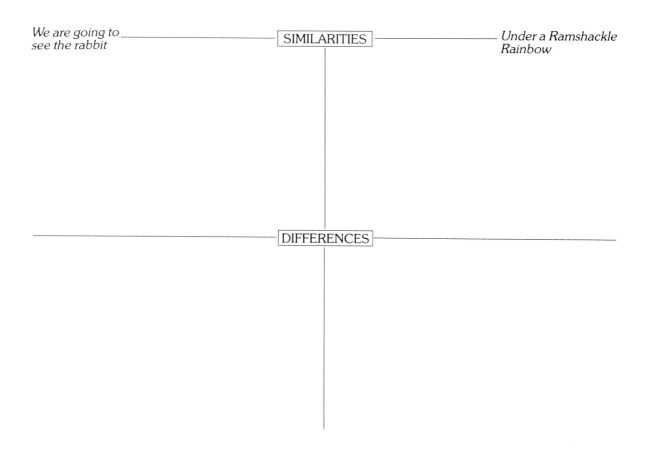

*We are going to see the rabbit* ———— SIMILARITIES ———— *Under a Ramshackle Rainbow*

DIFFERENCES

★ Invite all who feel able to write an extended piece with the title: *Similarities and Contrasts between the two poems* 'We are going to see the rabbit' *and* 'Under a Ramshackle Rainbow'.

★ Divide the class into small groups to plan an activity that they think will help another group to get into either of the poems.


## RELATED POEMS

(. . . that might, for some teachers and pupils, 'push out the boundaries'.)


'What We Said Sitting Making Fantasies' – James Berry *When I Dance* Puffin.
'The Sheepdog' – U. A. Fanthorpe *Selected Poems* King Penguin.
'Follower' – Seamus Heaney *Selected Poems 1965–75* Faber.
'Revelation' – Liz Lochhead in *Strictly Private* (ed. Roger McGough) Puffin Plus.
'Sir Patrick Spens' – Anon. See Related Poems, Section 5.

repeated hearings increase the pleasure

One characteristic of a good poem richly experienced is that it is memorable, and repeated hearings increase the pleasure. Another is that each repeated encounter is in some ways a new and potentially enriching experience: a recognition which underlies all of the poetry teaching suggested in this book. Each section has consequently proposed ways of working that involve repeated hearings and readings, leading to an accumulating store of known and remembered poems.

Children should frequently have a positive say in the content of sessions. It may arise from browsing amongst a collection of poetry books regularly available to them. But they might also be encouraged to make suggestions from their memory of enjoyed poems.

At least one of the teachers who has contributed to this book plans sequences of poetry sessions with the help of the full class.

## *SOME WAYS OF HEARING AGAIN*

★    Give a week's notice for groups of 3 or 4 to prepare a reading or presentation for a class poetry show. The poem(s) chosen should be one(s) encountered before but not yet presented by those in the group. You might restrict the choice to poems read in that particular term or year, or for a particular occasion.

★    Working on the rough calculation that 13/14 poems gives a programme lasting about 30–40 minutes, divide the class into groups, each to select and take responsibility for the presentation of 2, 3 or 4 poems of their own choosing. From these, assemble programmes that you can offer to other classes (maybe on an exchange basis) or a school assembly.

★    Divide the class into groups, each to prepare a 10/15 minute tape for the full class. As a preliminary discuss the qualities you would look for in a programme of poems to hold the attention of an audience of listeners. Time can be saved and possible tedium avoided by putting 3 or 4 groups together for the playback, with the task of selecting the one they judge best for playing to the full class.

★    Invite visitors to come and share some favourite poems with your class on a 'swop one for one' basis. Don't neglect the possible willingness of fathers, aunts, grandparents . . .

★    Select a number of familiar poems. Allocate each one to 2 or 3 different groups to prepare presentations, and arrange a performance when all the presentations can be viewed.

[This may be a joint activity with other classes. It worked very successfully across two different year groups in a primary school, involving 4 different classes: approximately 120 children. The contrasts between each of the presentations highlight ways in which valid responses to a poem may differ. This can lead later into discussion of the poem's most striking features which might include language, imagery, shape/structure, internal changes and patterns, or mood. As always, any technical terms used should be made clear as they are used.]

★    Make a group of children from the class responsible for the choice of poems to be used in a session.

★    Divide the class into groups. Pick a theme such as People, The Supernatural, Animals in the Wild, Feelings, Humour . . . Ask each group to find one or more poems on the chosen subject, which can later be shared by all and may be assembled into a class anthology.

★    Encourage requests for personal favourites at any time, or to include as additions in the course of regular poetry sessions. This is also a useful activity in those odd five minutes that need filling.

★    (cf. Kaye Webb's *I Like This Poem* Puffin)
Invite the class, in groups or individually, to compile an anthology of, say, 15–20 poems which they like, with a brief introduction about why each has been chosen. They will need to:
—   devise a selection procedure
—   discuss how to present it (book, taped anthology, performance . . .)
—   discuss how they will arrive at the final presentations.

PART TWO

*each group works out a
way of reading its verse*

## 1 BROWSING

If you have a good selection of attractive poetry books available (see Section III) provide frequent occasions for the class to dip into them. At times this may be individual and silent, at others they may find a different kind of enjoyment by working in pairs or threes, sharing poems or bits of poems that appeal.

Regular conclusions of browsing sessions might be exchanges of poems between groups, readings by single groups or individuals to the full class, suggestions of poems for looking at all together later, mini-anthologies on cassette . . .

The success of the time given to browsing depends heavily on *your* attitude towards it, the attitude you are striving to create towards poetry generally, and the quality of content and presentation/appearance of the books available. If it results in the class hearing pieces read by others who have sincerely found pleasure in them this is another valuable step towards a class which associates poetry with interest, pleasure and satisfaction.

## 2 CHOOSING POEMS

The introduction to each section attempts to make clear why the poems in the section have been chosen. But it may help to attempt some guidelines to apply whenever you are choosing.

Grabbing the nearest poem to hand, or one hastily recommended by a colleague, and taking it into the classroom in the hope that you will be inspired when you get there almost guarantees a boring poetry session.

Choice by the teacher or by children should come from the frequent browsing amongst a variety of poetry books: what's good for the pupil is good for the teacher. The ideal time – for excellent educational reasons – is when the pupils too are browsing (another possible application of time devoted to USSR – Uninterrupted, Sustained, Silent Reading – when everyone in the school is seen to be taking part).

There are many reasons for choosing a particular poem. They may be summed up as:
— you like it and want to read it to the class.
— you think, either rationally or instinctively, that the class will like it.
— it has some particular quality or subject matter that you want to introduce to the class, or which you feel they might enjoy, be stirred by, or otherwise respond to.
— it suggests to you a connection with some other activity, and you would like to pursue the connection.

If you still have problems in making choices some guiding principles might be:
— trust your own judgement.
— don't underestimate the children: they will sometimes astonish you by responding enthusiastically to a poem you find challenging. Nor do all the words in a poem have to be familiar.

— aim in the long term for a wide variety, including much that you consider slight but entertaining. Good diets include roughage!

And, very important:

— provide frequent occasions when the pupils themselves choose the poem. Poetry teaching is very much a matter of sharing personal enthusiasms.

## 3  READING A POEM

Let the poem tell you how it should be read. Be attentive to the voice(s) – or tones of voice – that you are hearing as you read it:

— is it serious, solemn, funny, outrageous, ironic . . . ?
— what sort of pace does it suggest?
— are there clear variations of any kind?

Play around with it until you can:

— feel the stresses.
— feel the rhythm.
— feel the pauses.

The aim of any reading should be to bring the poem alive for those listening by expressing *the reader's* sensitive and reflective experience of the poem. If others would read it differently the contrast/disagreement can in itself focus more attention on the poem. Every reading is an interpretation and one of the ways by which we can judge whether the reader has a sense of the poem *as a poem*, and not simply as words on paper.

It is for this reason that the teachers in this book make individual and group readings such a prominent feature of their poetry sessions. A group reading carries further the process of expressing the reader's experience of the poem by demanding that those reading come to some compromise or agreement before a reading satisfactory to them all can be achieved.

## 4  READING WITH A PARTNER

It is important to encourage concentrated private reading before the responses of others intrude too forcefully on an individual's response to a poem. But since there are those who find it hard to read silently and attentively, particularly when they have not chosen the reading matter, there is logic in suggesting that they may share a reading aloud with a partner, pausing whenever there is something they feel impelled to discuss.

## 5  DISCUSSION OF POEMS

The best questions for arousing discussion leave room for more than one answer and invite different viewpoints. Very often, as indicated in Part I, the most useful preliminary to full class discussion is small group discussion which enables the participants to express tentative responses and find ways of articulating their thoughts in a relatively relaxed situation. Early questions should be general and open:

— without looking back at the poem what do you remember about it?
— are there any words or lines that you can recall?
— were there any pictures that it brought into your mind?
— supposing you wanted to tell someone what this poem was about. What would you say? Try it with the person sitting next to you.

As the discussion gets going allow it to develop a momentum and a direction of its own. If it is slow to do this, allow time for reading it again. If it still fails, don't labour it.

You may have clear directions in your head that you feel the class must follow before they can be said to have really come to grips with the poem. *Don't rush these.* It is important that they move at their own pace in the early stages, which is the purpose of the activities following on from the first encounters.

It is likely that you will have your own views of what is of central interest in the poem, but once you declare these with any suggestion of authority you run the risk of excluding other readings which, for others, may reveal the real heart of the poem. Even when you feel that certain lines hold *the key* to the poem (as you might, for instance, with the closing lines in 'A Case of Murder' page 64) aim to give the class time and space to discover this for themselves rather than stating it as an unquestionable fact. If some resist such a suggestion to the end, better leave it at that than give the impression that you see yourself as the final authority on the 'real' meaning of poems.

Once the class come to think *that*, it will be the end of comfortable and open discussion.

## 6  JOTTING

Common to all ages is the difficulty of knowing what you want to say until you have said it, and knowing what you want to write until you have written it. Making jottings can help. It records tentative insights, which do not necessarily make obvious sense, but may later be the basis of complete and articulate thoughts and statements. Unless they are recorded they easily get lost in the process of shaping and making publicly acceptable.

The rules are simple: the jotter writes down words, phrases, snatches of thought, feelings, as they occur, and without editing. In relation to a poem this may accompany the act of listening to the poem being read (and, possibly, re-read) or may take place in a prescribed silence following a reading. It should be preferably before other people's judgements and reactions can have influence.

This provides a basis for subsequent writing or discussion in which the personal and initial response may be preserved. It also provides a foundation for positive participation in these activities.

116

As indicated in Part One Section 5, some jottings may be expressed through signs, lines, loops, and colours more efficiently and economically than through words.

## 7 LEARNING 'BY HEART'

There are still many teachers, not yet retired, who were at school when learning by heart was highly regarded as an educational process.

There is a strong argument that people should be free to choose what they learn, but few – I suspect – would doubt the value of carrying throughout life remembered words, poems, passages from books, parts in plays . . .

I can't actually think of anything I have learnt by heart that I *regret* learning, so there may even be justification in a teacher suggesting to a class the poems that might be learnt. The learning by heart, of suggested poems or self-selected poems, is giving the learner an ever available source of pleasure, and, possibly, inspiration.

An approach to poetry teaching which provides opportunities for performance and presentation gives a natural outlet for any poems learnt in this way. Anyone who has enjoyed a presentation by poets such as Benjamin Zephaniah, Roger McGough or John Agard will need no persuading about the added impact of a poem spoken rather than read.

## 8 IMAGINATION AND CONCENTRATION

In a number of sections the suggestion is made that the teacher should stimulate the imaginations of the pupils and encourage concentration before introducing a poem or asking them to write or talk. One effective way of doing this is for the teacher to talk them into a mood appropriate for meeting the poem with a sequence of 'leads'.

Supposing, for example, that you are wanting them to think about an imaginary or real character to write or talk about, maybe as a prelude to a group of poems about unconventional characters. You might begin by asking them to close their eyes and let their thoughts flow as you talk them through the creation or recall of the character, allowing thinking time between each instruction for their imaginations to work. For example:
You are looking at the door of this person's home from the outside.
— What strikes you most about it?
— What colour is it?
— How big is it?
— Look to one side of it. What is there?
— Now look to the other side.
— Look above it.
Now the door is opening and the person you are thinking about is coming out. Look closely.
— What is the most striking thing about them?

117

—  About how old?
—  How dressed? Look closely and in detail, from head to feet.
—  They are carrying something. What is it?

The person is walking away from the house now, as quickly as they are able. How do they walk?

Imagine that you can see their face, very closely. Does anything in the expression give you a clue about why they are in such a hurry?

This is a powerful technique, not only for working on the imagination but also for drawing on real memories or for speculating about the future, as, for example, in Stage 1 of the second Encounter on page 103.

## 9  ROUTINES

Certain activities in Poetry sessions are quite regular – to do with listening, watching, presenting, showing. A great deal of time is saved if you establish agreed and respected routines which not only help the speed and efficiency with which these activities take place, but also demonstrate quite positively the value you place on what is happening. Once you have agreed on the routines they need to be followed consistently.

## 10  PRESENTATION

The preparation of a poem for presentation to other people is not only an enjoyable classroom activity, but also a way into appreciation of that poem for both the presenters and the audience.

Once established as a classroom activity it needs little prompting and the variations from simple to complex seem endless.

A pupil who has found a poem and wants to read it to someone else is offering the simplest form of presentation. At the other extreme is the full class presentation of a programme of varied poems which all have helped to select, prepare and take part in. This might include a combination of drama, movement, mime, art, music and so on. The audience in this case may be another class, the whole school, or even another school with which an exchange of poetry entertainment has been arranged.

Some variables should be encouraged as a matter of policy. Everyone at some time might perhaps experience the responsibility of preparing a solo or group presentation for a small audience. If some find it easier when the audience is invisible, a tape recording may serve. Another important variable is choosing the poem. There are positive gains in expecting pupils to find poems to work on for presentation. It is an occasion for browsing and making choices. If they are in groups, it is an occasion for purposeful discussion. But there are also occasions when there is real value in working on a poem selected by someone else. It is exciting, for example, for a group to be given a poem with a set time allowed for preparing a presentation, knowing that each of the other groups has been given a different poem and that all will come together in a miniature poetry show when the time runs out.

## 11 MULTIPLE VOICES AND CHORAL SPEECH

The close link between poetry and music can often be most effectively highlighted in a reading through the use of more than a single voice. A regular task could be to ask groups of three or four to work on a single poem to produce a reading which includes all of their voices which is 'true' to the sense and the feeling of the poem. Over a period of time the class can explore the wide variety of ways voices can be combined to create a good reading: separate individual voices, a combination of separate and group voices, voices in unison, voices out of time, voices which echo, and so on.

Choral speech takes this activity further and draws on techniques associated with drama, movement, mime, music, mask-making and 'theatre' generally. It can be simple or complicated, but in either case the preparation is all-important. There is an example of a script prepared both for a simple and for an elaborate performance in Part I, Section 8.

## 12 DRAMA

There are basic drama activities which any interested teacher can manage quite readily. All of the following are valuable for exploring poetry.

**i** *Improvisation*: bringing alive through characterisation, interaction, movement. Appropriate subjects are the conflicts within the poem (such as Dick, the boys and the Aunt and Uncle in 'Dick Lander') or the context in which a poem is set (such as a deserted house in the middle of a forest). Judge the success of the improvisation by the conviction and imagination with which the pupils create the scene and their own part in it. Encourage them to comment on and evaluate the work of other groups.

**ii** *Still Pictures/Photographs*: a frozen moment from the poem created as a photographer would compose his picture. One member of the group may well take charge as the photographer. The aim is for a two-dimensional effect and they should be judged accordingly.

**iii** *Tableaux/Sculptures*: a different form of frozen moment – the work of a sculptor rather than a photographer. As before, a member of the group might take on that role and manipulate the others as clay. The visual impression should be considered from all angles and the viewers invited to walk around.

**iv** *Freezing*: a technique for stopping dramatic actions at a signal from the person in control. Very useful for deepening concentration and examin-

119

ing critically details of the drama or improvisation at a particular moment: facial expression, posture, movement, and so on.

**v** *Slow Motion*: a technique for focussing attention, particularly useful to restore concentration when the dramatic work is sloppy or thoughtless. A means of exploring such things as how movements develop and how the body externally reflects inner experience.

## 13 ROLE PLAY

Role play involves one or more members of a group taking on an assumed character. This has proved an immensely powerful activity for exploring fictional, historical or mythical characters and situations.

In teaching poetry it can give a sharp focus to the exploration of a poem. The teacher or another invited adult may 'go into role' as a character in the poem (a member of the family that owned the dog in 'Praise of a Collie', a local villager in 'Sensemaya') to be questioned by the class. A further stage may take the whole class into role. 'Big' poems, such as 'The Highwayman' or 'The Pied Piper' as well as short poems such as 'Dick Lander' can bring various individuals and groups within a community together through role play for examination of the events and the situations told directly and by implication in the poem. The photograph on page 21 shows two pupils in role. One is a tenant threatened with eviction and the other a representative from the local council exploring the situation in 'This Letter's to Say'. A stage further might involve a protest meeting of all the tenants under threat, together with a group of council officials, newspaper reporters and other interested people involving the whole class and the teacher in role.

It is important that everyone taking part, in role or not, agrees to suspend disbelief for as long as the role play is going on. Very simple props or an item of clothing can help to 'create' the sense of character and identity. (Christine Hall offers some advice about this on page 62.) But all that is absolutely necessary is that those taking part understand and co-operate in whatever takes place, and that they have – knowingly or unknowingly – been prepared for it.

Role play may last for anything from 5 minutes to 45 minutes, or you might return to it on different occasions over a week or so. The duration is most often decided by how absorbed the group or class becomes. Whatever the length of time, there needs to be opportunity afterwards to exchange ideas and opinions arising from what has taken place.

## 14 HOT-SEATING

This is a specific use of role play in which an individual, or a group speaking collectively as one individual, can be questioned in role by the rest of the class. When this is carefully prepared – by those in the hot-seat previously considering very closely all that they know or can deduce about the character

120

they represent, and anticipating likely questions – it can be a dramatic and absorbing way of exploring character, motivation and situation. (After looking at a number of poems by a single author the person hot-seated might be in-role as the poet.)

The rule is that those in the hot-seat speak for the character they represent in answer to any questions they are asked by those not in the hot-seat. But they can only answer according to what they know or can deduce from the sources of information available to them, or what is *consistent* with those sources.

## 15 BRAINSTORMING

A tactic for freeing the normal inhibitions of discussion – the agreement is that people call out whatever comes into their heads in relation to a given topic, without being deterred by anxieties about relevance, importance or sounding silly. The result should be a blitz of thoughts, ideas, words which are recorded, possibly on the board or on a large sheet of paper, as a base for subsequent talking, discussion, or writing about the topic.

## 16 DRAWING AND PAINTING

Some pupils choose to illustrate a part of a poem or a feeling it conveys without prompting. Sometimes you may propose this as a way of exploring the poem.

Provide as wide a range of materials as possible and encourage the pupils to consider the suitability of the materials they select, and to be prepared to explain their choices. Whenever possible make time for the final products to be displayed and for those responsible to talk about them.

Working in groups of two or three requires discussion about the poem and the illustration to reach decisions which will be acceptable to all of them. Ideally, the activity of drawing and/or painting will be collaborative too. Ensure that there is time for them to produce a piece of work which satisfies them all.

Resist the temptation to fill in a final five minutes after a poetry reading with 'drawing a picture' unless you intend the drawings to be preliminary sketches or a means of holding first responses.

The photograph on page 123 shows the work on 'Overheard in a Saltmarsh' by a group of 9–11 year olds in a Devon primary school. The separate pictures were prepared as graphics to accompany a reading of the poem for 'televising' (with the help of two students on teaching practice, one enthusiastic teacher and a portable video camera). The full sequence has 16 illustrations: a mixture of paint and collage which incorporates various materials to produce a 3-dimensional effect. Apart from its worth as a carefully considered and organised group-response to a poem it is an excellent example of a poem 'translated' into a different medium.

121

## OVERHEARD ON A SALTMARSH

Nymph, nymph, what are your beads?
Green glass, goblin. Why do you stare at them?
Give them me.
                    No.
Give them me. Give them me.
                              No.
Then I will howl all night in the reeds,
Lie in the mud and howl for them.
Goblin, why do you love them so?
They are better than stars or water,
Better than voices of winds that sing,
Better than any man's fair daughter,
Your green glass beads on a silver ring.
Hush, I stole them out of the moon.
Give me your beads, I desire them.
                              No.
I will howl in a deep lagoon
For your green glass beads, I love them so.
Give them me. Give them.
                         No.


*Harold Monro*


## 17 POSTERS

Poems and poets lend themselves to posters which incorporate words and images that reinforce the words. The aim is to produce an informative poster which tells the viewer as much as possible about the poem or the poet. Every aspect of the work should be chosen consciously to suit the subject, including the colours and materials used.

As a small group activity the process itself generates discussion. The end products can also be a focus for subsequent discussion as those who have worked on the posters explain the decisions that they had to make. The level of interest and anticipation can be raised by inviting a visitor to view the resulting display and to join in questioning the groups about their posters.

The kind of questions asked might be:
— how did you begin?
— what decisions did you make before you began?
— how did you divide up the work?
— what does your poster tell the viewer about the poem if they haven't read it (or, the poet, if they haven't read her or him)?
— was there anything you disagreed about?

122

*Introductory illustration*

*Title illustration*

*Nymph, nymph, what are your beads?*

*They are better than stars or water*

*Hush, I stole them out of the moon*

*Better than voices of winds that sing*

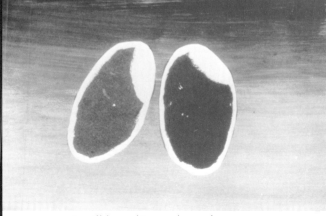

*I will howl in a deep lagoon*

*Give them me. Give them. No.*

## 18 COLLAGE

Collage is a powerful medium for those who are diffident about their ability to draw or to paint to their own satisfaction. It requires just as much thought and careful selection of appropriate images and, where relevant, words. The impact of the finished product and its success in representing the poem or the poets can be just as great. Again the person or groups responsible should be given opportunity to talk about what they have done and the decisions they had to make.

Other forms of collage are equally interesting, demanding and powerful in their effect.

Word collages are constructed from quotations of extracts or individual words taken from the subject of the collage – in our case a poem or a group of poems. For display, a word collage can be produced on card, often incorporating significant use of colour and visual images. But just as *effectively* a word collage can be produced on a cassette, possibly incorporating other sounds.

Yet another form of collage is the sound collage. For this the sounds are either improvised from available materials or made up of snippets of recognizable music.

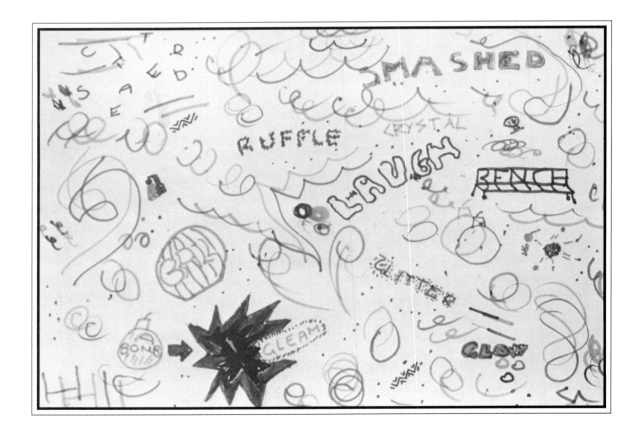

## 19  MAKING MASKS

There is a wide range of materials helpful in mask making: newspapers, cardboard boxes, cereal boxes, tissue paper, a range of fabrics and colours, elastic, string, cotton wool, poster paints, spray paints . . . A cover for the floor is generally a necessary preliminary.

For those who have no experience Maria Hussey suggests two simple models which she has used in school:

### i  *Brown Paper Masks*

Wrap a piece of brown paper that is approximately twice the length of the head around the head of your model and pull tight. Then stick the two edges together with masking tape. Mark the point where the model's eyes and mouth come. Remove the mask and cut out eyes and mouth to required shape. Create hair by cutting the paper into strips and curling with scissors. Use the masking tape to attach other features, such as eyebrows.

### ii  *Paper Shape Masks*

Fold a piece of stiff card in half. Draw the required shape onto one side of the card – starting and ending at the central fold. Measure the position of the wearer's eyes and mark on the mask. Cut out the shape and the eye holes. Add other features if required. The mask can be mounted either by fixing onto a stick, securing with ties like spectacles, or attaching to a paper head-band.

## 20  SHARPENING IMAGES

More than once in this book there is the suggestion that a class should explore a poem by means of some rapid sketches, one of which is then selected for polishing and sharpening. (A close colleague is still showing overheads made from the first time we tried this, in an Exeter High School nearly ten years ago. The poem was Wilfred Owen's 'Dulce et Decorum Est' and the overheads have been shown on Summer Schools and Courses all round the world. This remains for both of us a highly regarded technique for engaging with a strongly visual poem.)

The stage of sharpening the final image is important and may need explanation. It needs to be discussed with the class before they go on to this stage. One poem for which this activity is suggested is 'Hedgehog' in Part I, Section 3.

Suppose a girl has chosen for polishing and sharpening an illustration for the lines:

> . . . his pointed face
> Is furry and his soft black leather snout
> Gentle and wrinkled.

She has produced a sketch of a hedgehog on a patch of garden. If she thinks about it, the quotation is simply about *the hedgehog's head*, so her sketch might be better without either his body or the garden. She might even decide that the head is too much – all that is wanted is the hedgehog's face and snout, possibly from a different angle, along with the quotation.

Apart from the preliminary discussion about this process, it is yet another activity which is a potentially lively focus for discussion and display when it is completed.

## 21  WRITING POETRY

It would be a strange exploration of poetry which did not provide frequent opportunities and encouragement for those taking part to *write* poetry themselves.

Many teachers, myself included, still regard *Poetry in the Making*, by Ted Hughes, as the most helpful book on the subject, because it explores *what poetry is* and *how poetry is written* in terms accessible to children, and avoids any suggestion that a poem is simply a matter of pattern and form.

Since *Poetry in the Making* was published, many more books about writing poetry have been written, many of them rich in ideas and approaches, many based on experience both of teaching and of writing poetry very successfully.

I have listed in Part III a number of books by such well qualified people, which deal specifically with stimulating and helping children to write poetry.

PART THREE

One way of generating enthusiasm for poems is to have a large number and a wide range of stimulating and attractive poetry books around. In school a *portable* collection of 35–45 books in a box or a case can be used by several classes. It leads naturally to browsing, choosing, rejecting, selecting for personal anthologies, sharing personal stories, and articulating reasons for likes and dislikes.

The following lists are guides to some of the poetry books available for the Primary and Lower Secondary age range. They are grouped in collections in the hope that schools may have funds to put together *at least* one portable poetry box. Each collection draws from the full range of poetry available and caters for a wide range of tastes.

\*    signifies that a paperback edition is available.

# A COLLECTION OF POETRY BOOKS FOR 8–13

## I

*Slanted towards the younger end: chosen with consideration for what poetry*
*they may already have experienced. Appropriate too as a first introduction.*

| | | | |
|---|---|---|---|
| 1 | *The Mighty Slide** | Alan Ahlberg | Puffin |
| 2 | *Please Mrs Butler** | Allan Ahlberg | Puffin |
| 3 | *Say it Again, Granny** | John Agard | Bodley Head |
| 4 | *Oxford Book of Poetry for Children** | Edward Blishen | O.U.P. |
| 5 | *Animals Like Us** | Tony Bradman | Puffin |
| 6 | *Figgie Hobbin** | Charles Causley | Puffin |
| 7 | *Early in the Morning** | Charles Causley | Puffin |
| 8 | *The Tail of the Trinosaur** | Charles Causley | Puffin |
| 9 | *Standing on a Strawberry** | John Cunliffe | Deutsch |
| 10 | *Around the World in Eighty Poems** | J & G Curry | Beaver |
| 11 | *Wry Rhymes for Troublesome Times** | Max Fatchen | Puffin |
| 12 | *Invitation to a Mouse** | Eleanor Farjeon | Knight |
| 13 | *A First Poetry Book** | John Foster | O.U.P. |
| 14 | *A Second Poetry Book** | John Foster | O.U.P. |
| 15 | *A Puffin Book of Verse** | Eleanor Graham | Puffin |
| 16 | *Of Caterpillars, Cats and Cattle** | Ann Harvey | Puffin |
| 17 | *Island of the Children** | Angela Huth | Orchard |
| 18 | *Hiawatha* | Henry Wadsworth Longfellow (ill. Susan Jeffers) | Hamish Hamilton |
| 19 | *Hiawatha's Childhood* | Henry Wadsworth Longfellow (ill. Errol Le Cain) | Faber |
| 20 | *A Flock of Words* | David Mackay | Faber |
| 21 | *The Witch's Brew & Other Poems** | Wes Magee | C.U.P. |
| 22 | *A Calendar of Poems* | Wes Magee | Bodley Head |
| 23 | *Secret Laughter** | Walter de la Mare | Puffin |
| 24 | *An Imaginary Menagerie** | Roger McGough | Puffin |
| 25 | *Boo to a Goose** | John Mole | Peterloo Poets |
| 26 | *Custard and Company** | Ogden Nash | Puffin |
| 27 | *Poetry Jump-Up** | Grace Nichols | Puffin |
| 28 | *The Puffin Book of Nursery Rhymes** | Iona & Peter Opie | Puffin |
| 29 | *Sing a Song of Popcorn* | B. Schenk de Regnier | Hodder & Stoughton |
| 30 | *Don't Put Mustard in the Custard** | Michael Rosen | Armada |
| 31 | *Wouldn't You Like to Know?** | Michael Rosen | Puffin |
| 32 | *Have You Heard the Sun Singing?* | Adrian Rumble | Evans |

| 33 | The Clever Potato* | Vernon Scannell | Beaver |
| 34 | How Does It Feel? | David Scott | Blackie |
| 35 | A Light in the Attic | Shel Silverstein | Cape |
| 36 | A Child's Garden of Verses* | Robert Louis Stevenson | O.U.P. |
| 37 | All Sorts of Poems* | Ann Thwaite | Magnet |
| 38 | Our Village | John Yeoman | Walker |
| 39 | Conkers | Barrie Wade | O.U.P. |
| 40 | Wild Poems | Daisy Wallace | Bell & Hyman |
| 41 | The Puffin Book of Funny Verse* | Julia Watson | Puffin |
| 42 | I Like This Poem* | Kaye Webb | Puffin |
| 43 | The Magic Tree* | David Woolger | O.U.P. |
| 44 | Poems for 9 year olds and under* | Kit Wright | Puffin |
| 45 | Rabbiting On* | Kit Wright | Young Lions |

# A COLLECTION OF POETRY BOOKS FOR 8–13

## II

*Slanted towards the older end: chosen with consideration for what poetry they will go on to experience in the future, if they are lucky.*

| 1 | Watchwords One* | Michael & Peter Benton | Hodder & Stoughton |
| 2 | Watchwords Two* | Michael & Peter Benton | Hodder & Stoughton |
| 3 | When I Dance* | James Berry | Puffin |
| 4 | Penguin Book of Caribbean Verse* | Paula Burnett | Penguin |
| 5 | Collected Poems 1951–75* | Charles Causley | Macmillan |
| 6 | A Field of Vision | Charles Causley | Macmillan |
| 7 | Secret as Toads | Leonard Clark | Chatto & Windus |
| 8 | The Corn Growing | Leonard Clark | Hodder & Stoughton |
| 9 | The Rhyme of the Ancient Mariner* | S.T. Coleridge (ill. Gustave Doré) | Dover |
| 10 | Tog the Ribber or Granny's Tale | Paul Coltman and Gillian McClure | Deutsch |
| 11 | Selected poems 1923–1958* | e. e. cummings | Faber |
| 12 | The New Wind Has Wings: Poems from Canada | M. Downie and B. Robertson | O.U.P. |

| 13 | Growltiger's Last Stand and other poems | T. S. Eliot | Faber |
|----|----|----|----|
| 14 | The Learned Hippopotamus* | Gavin Ewart | Beaver |
| 15 | Something I Remember* | Eleanor Farjeon | Puffin |
| 16 | A Third Poetry Book* | John Foster | O.U.P. |
| 17 | A Fourth Poetry Book* | John Foster | O.U.P. |
| 18 | Third Time Lucky* | Mick Gowar | Viking Kestrel |
| 19 | Six of the Best* | Ann Harvey | Puffin |
| 20 | The New Dragon Book of Verse | M. Harrison & C. Stuart Clark | O.U.P. |
| | | | |
| 21 | What is Truth?* | Ted Hughes | Faber |
| 22 | The Earth Owl and Other People | Ted Hughes | Faber |
| 23 | The Rattlebag* | Ted Hughes and Seamus Heaney | Faber |
| | | | |
| 24 | The Curse of the Vampire Socks | Terry Jones | Pavilion |
| 25 | Poems* | Katherine Mansfield | O.U.P. |
| 26 | Peacock Pie* | Walter de la Mare | Faber |
| 27 | Strictly Private* | Roger McGough | Puffin |
| 28 | Startling Verse for all the Family* | Spike Milligan | Puffin |
| 29 | Midnight Forest* | Judith Nicholls | Faber |
| 30 | Magic Mirror and Other Poems for Children* | Judith Nicholls | Faber |
| 31 | Under Another Sky | Alastair Niven | Carcanet |
| 32 | The Highwayman* | Alfred Noyes (ill. Charles Keeping) | O.U.P. |
| | | | |
| 33 | The Bed Book* | Sylvia Plath | Faber |
| 34 | Ten Golden Years | C. Powling and S. Grindley | Walker |
| | | | |
| 35 | The Wolfhound Book of Irish Poems* | Bridie Quinn & Seamus Cashman | Wolfhound Press |
| | | | |
| 36 | Goblin Market* | Christina Rossetti | Harrap |
| 37 | Catch the Light | Vernon Scannell, Gregory Harrison & Lawrence Smith | O.U.P. |
| | | | |
| 38 | Selected Poems* | Stevie Smith | Penguin |
| 39 | Selected Poems* | Edward Thomas | Faber |
| 40 | First Draft* | Nika Turbina | Marion Boyars |
| 41 | Golden Apples* | Fiona Waters | Piper Books |
| 42 | Nine O'Clock Bell* | Raymond Wilson | Puffin |
| 43 | Poems for 10 year olds and over* | Kit Wright | Puffin |
| 44 | Poems 1974–83* | Kit Wright | Hutchinson |

# A COLLECTION OF POETRY BOOKS FOR 8–13

## III

*Chosen with no other consideration than appropriateness across this full age range.*

| | | | |
|---|---|---|---|
| 1 | *The Faber Book of Children's Verse** | Janet Adam Smith | Faber |
| 2 | *I Din Do Nuttin and Other Poems** | John Agard | Magnet |
| 3 | *Heard it in the Playground** | Allan Ahlberg | Viking Kestrel |
| 4 | *Selected Cautionary Verses** | Hilaire Belloc | Puffin |
| 5 | *Jabberwocky and Other Poems** | Lewis Carroll | Hodder & Stoughton |
| 6 | *The Puffin Book of Magic Verse** | Charles Causley | Puffin |
| 7 | *Jack the Treacle Eater** | Charles Causley | Macmillan |
| 8 | *The Jungle Sale* | June Crebbin | Viking Kestrel |
| 9 | *Down Our Street** | J. and G. Curry | Magnet |
| 10 | *Revolting Rhymes** | Roald Dahl | Picture Puffin |
| 11 | *Tails with a Twist* | Alfred Douglas | Batsford |
| 12 | *Whispers from a Wardrobe* | Richard Edwards | Lutterworth |
| 13 | *The Illustrated Old Possum** | T. S. Eliot | Faber |
| 14 | *What a lot of nonsense!** | John Foster | Robert Royce |
| 15 | *School's Out!** | John Foster | O.U.P. |
| 16 | *Rhinestone Rhino* | Adrian Henri | Methuen |
| 17 | *Someone is Flying Balloons: Australian Poems for Children* | Jill Heylen & Celia Jellett | C.U.P. |
| 18 | *Come Hither** | Walter de la Mare | Puffin |
| 19 | *Ducks and Dragons** | Gene Kemp | Puffin |
| 20 | *A Book of Bosh** | Edward Lear | Puffin |
| 21 | *The Children's Book of Children's Rhymes** | Christopher Logue | Piccolo |
| 22 | *The Penguin Book of Animal Verse** | George MacBeth | Penguin |
| 23 | *Morning Break & Other Poems** | Wes Magee | C.U.P. |
| 24 | *Madtail, Miniwhale and Other Shape Poems* | Wes Magee | Viking Kestrel |
| 25 | *Nonstop Nonsense** | Margaret Mahy | Magnet |
| 26 | *You Tell Me** | Roger McGough & Michael Rosen | Puffin |
| 27 | *Nailing the Shadow** | Roger McGough | Puffin |
| 28 | *Sky in the Pie** | Roger McGough | Puffin |
| 29 | *Silly Verse for Kids** | Spike Milligan | Puffin |
| 30 | *Strawberry Drums* | Adrian Mitchell | Macdonald/ Purnell |
| 31 | *Nothingmas Day** | Adrian Mitchell | Allison & Busby |
| 32 | *Come Into My Tropical Garden* | Grace Nichols | A & C Black |
| 33 | *The Oxford Book of Children's Verse* | Iona & Peter Opie | O.U.P. |

| 34 | *Salford Road** | Gareth Owen | Young Lions |
|----|----|----|----|
| 35 | *The Walker Book of Poetry for Children* | J. Prelutsky and A. Lobel | Walker |
| 36 | *Complete Poems for Children* | James Reeves | Heinemann |
| 37 | *The Wandering Moon and Other Poems** | James Reeves | Puffin |
| 38 | *Mind Your Own Business** | Michael Rosen | Young Lions |
| 39 | *Welcome, and other Poems* | Geoffrey Summerfield | Deutsch |
| 40 | *Skipping to Babylon* | Carol Tate | O.U.P. |
| 41 | *Witch Poems* | D. Wallace | Pepper Press |
| 42 | *Giant Poems* | D. Wallace | Pepper Press |
| 43 | *Every Poem Tells a Story** | Raymond Wilson | Viking Kestrel |
| 44 | *The Magic Tree: Poems of Fantasy and Mystery** | David Woolger | O.U.P. |
| 45 | *Hot Dog** | Kit Wright | Puffin |

## SOME BOOKS ABOUT WRITING POETRY

| *Into Poetry* | Richard Andrews | Ward Lock |
|----|----|----|
| *Does It Have to Rhyme?** | Sandy Brownjohn | Hodder & Stoughton |
| *What Rhymes With Secret?** | Sandy Brownjohn | Hodder & Stoughton |
| *Meet and Write*, Books 1 and 2 | Sandy & Alan Brownjohn | Hodder & Stoughton |
| *Poetry Writing in the Primary School** | Pie Corbett | Kent Reading and Language Development Centre, North Holmes Road, Canterbury, Kent CT1 1GU |
| *In Tune With Yourself* | Jennifer Dunn, Morag Styles & Nick Warburton | C.U.P. |
| *Writing Poems** | Michael Harrison & C. Stuart Clark | O.U.P. |
| *Poetry in the Making** | Ted Hughes | Faber |
| *Creative Writing for Juniors* | Barry Maybury | Batsford |
| *There's a poet behind you* | Morag Styles & Helen Cook | A. & C. Black |

| *I see a voice\** | Michael Rosen | Hutchinson |
| *An Early Start to Poetry* | Colin Walker | Macdonald Educational |

## PARTICULARLY USEFUL FOR REFERENCES

| *Where's that Poem?\** | Helen Morris | Blackwell |
| (Revised edition 1990) | | |

## USEFUL ADDRESSES FOR INFORMATION, NEWS AND MATERIALS ABOUT POETRY FOR SCHOOLS

*The Poetry Society*, 21 Earls Court Square, London SW5 9DE
(A wide range of services promoting poetry, including the *Poets in School* Scheme, Teachers' Information Sheets, regular newsletters and annual competitions.)

*The Poetry Library*, Level 5, Red Side, Royal Festival Hall, London, SE1.
('The most comprehensive and accessible collection of twentieth century poetry in Britain . . . including poetry for children.')

*Books for Keeps*, 6 Brightfield Road, Lee, London, SE12 8QF.
(Six issues a year which cover the whole range of children's literature. Publishers of the most comprehensive list of books relating to children's poetry and poetry teaching available: *Poetry 0–16*. It says enough about each book for you to decide whether it will meet your needs.)

For materials previously published by *ILEA Learning Materials Service*:
Harcourt Brace Jovanovich Ltd., Foots Cray High Street, Sidcup, Kent DA14 5HP (081-267-4466)

## ACKNOWLEDGEMENTS

We wish to thank the following authors, agents and publishers for permission to reproduce copyright poems:

Edward Kamau Brathwaite and Oxford University Press for 'Cat' from *Other Exiles* by Edward Kamau Brathwaite (1975) © Oxford University Press (1975)

Alan Brownjohn and Hutchinson Ltd for 'We are going to see the rabbit' from *Collected Poems*

Charles Causley, David Higham Associates and Macmillan Publishers Ltd for 'By St Thomas Water' and 'Riley' from *Collected Poems*, 'Maggie Dooley' from *Jack the Treacle Eater*, 'Dick Lander' from *A Field of Vision*; and the author, agent and Viking Kestrel for 'The Money Came In, Came In' from *Early in the Morning*

The Literary Trustees of Walter de la Mare and the Society of Authors as their representative for 'Some One', 'The House' and 'The Listeners' by Walter de la Mare

Gregory Harrison for 'Posting Letters' from *Posting Letters* published by Oxford University Press

Miroslav Holub, his translators and Penguin Books for 'Fairy Tale' from *Miroslav Holub: Selected Poems* translated by Ian Milner and George Theiner. Reproduced by permission of Penguin Books Ltd

Margaret Mahy and J M Dent & Sons for 'The Tin Can Band' from *The Second Margaret Mahy Storybook*

Normal MacCaig and Chatto & Windus Ltd for 'Praise of a Collie' from *Selected Poems*

The author and Spike Milligan Productions Ltd for 'New Members Welcome' by Spike Milligan

Lilian Moore and Marian Reiner for 'Until I Saw the Sea' from *I Feel The Same Way* © 1967 by Lilian Moore. Reprinted by permission of Marian Reiner for the author

Grace Nichols and Curtis Brown Group Ltd on behalf of the author for 'I'm a Parrot'

Clive Sansom and David Higham Associates Ltd for 'Hedgehog' from *An English Year* published by Chatto & Windus

Vernon Scannell and Robson Books Ltd for 'A Case of Murder'

James MacGibbon for 'The Singing Cat' by Stevie Smith from *The Collected Poems of Stevie Smith* published by Penguin Books (20th Century Classics)

Gareth Owen and Rogers, Coleridge and White Ltd for 'Winter' from *Salford Road* © 1976 by Gareth Owen, published by Kestrel Books 1979

Hal Summers and Oxford University Press for 'Out of School' from *Tomorrow is My Love* by Hal Summers (1978) © Hal Summers 1978

Nika Turbina, her translators and Marion Boyars Publications Ltd for 'The Voice' and 'I'll be lost in the fog', translated by Antonina Bouis; and 'I want kindness', 'Don't Listen to Lamp Posts' and 'The Doll', translated by Elaine Feinstein, from *First Draft*: Poems by Nika Turbina, with an introduction by Yevgeny Yevtushenko and translations by Antonina W Bouis and Elaine Feinstein. Published by Marion Boyars, London and New York 1988

Mrs A M Walsh for 'The Bully Asleep' by John Walsh from *The Roundabout by the Sea* published by Oxford University Press

Raymond Wilson and Faber & Faber Ltd for 'This Letter's to Say' from *Daft Davy*; Raymond Wilson and John Murray Ltd for 'Old Johnny Armstrong' from *Poems Old and New*